BURPEE   AMERICAN   GARDENING   SERIES

GARDEN DESIGNS

BURPEE

AMERICAN GARDENING SERIES

GARDEN DESIGNS

Alice Recknagel Ireys

PRENTICE
HALL
PRESS

New York ◆ *London* ◆ *Toronto* ◆ *Sydney* ◆ *Tokyo* ◆ *Singapore*

Cover: A portion of the garden, "An Island of Fragrance" (page 15).
Preceding pages: The casual glory of this mass planting belies the thoughtful, though easy, design. Stately dahlias, foreground, stand against a lush background of the mixed colors of cosmos 'Sensation'.

 PRENTICE HALL PRESS
15 Columbus Circle
New York, NY 10023

Copyright © 1991 by W. Atlee Burpee & Company

PRENTICE HALL PRESS and colophon are registered trademarks of Simon & Schuster, Inc.

Designed by Patricia Fabricant
Manufactured in the United States of America

First Edition January 1991

Burpee is a registered trademark of W. Atlee Burpee & Company.

I wish to thank Suzie Bales for her inspiration and help in putting these gardens together.

I want to express appreciation to Susan Littlefield, Sandra Ross and George Salley for their assistance in various stages of the plans and write-ups.

Many thanks to the Burpee staff for their help: Jan Garrigan and Al Scheider in copy-editing; horticulturists Chela Kleiber, Charles Cresson, Steve Frowine and Carol Whitenack; and photography supervisor Barbara Wolverton.

Photography Credits:

Agricultural Research Service, USDA
All-America Rose Selections, Inc.
Bales, Suzanne Frutig
Bodger Seeds, Ltd.
Cresson, Charles O.
Dibblee, Steven
Frowine, Steven A.
Gitts, Nicholas of Swan Island Dahlias
Horticultural Photography, Corvallis, Oregon
International Bloembollen Centrum
Kurt Bluemel, Inc.
Rokach, Allen
Van der Salm Bulbfarm, Inc.
Viette, Andre

Watercolor illustrations: Jean LaRue
Garden design plans: Richard Gambier

Library of Congress Cataloging-in-Publication Data

Ireys, Alice Recknagel.
    Burpee American gardening series. Garden designs / Alice
Ireys.
        p.   cm.
    ISBN 0-13-093345-7 : $7.95
    1. Gardens—Designs and plans. I. Title. II. Title: Garden
design.
SB473.I68 1991
    712'.6—dc20   90-34677
                                                          CIP

CONTENTS

Introduction   7

Helpful Hints   9

Annual Flower Gardens   11
  An Easy, Carefree Garden   12
  An Island of Fragrance   15
  Crescents of Color   17
  A Yellow and Blue Crescent   18
  A Blue Crescent   20
  A Pink Crescent   22
  A Cutting Garden   24
  A Garden of Annual Everlastings   27
  A Rainbow of Impatiens   29
  Marigolds by the Back Door   30

Bulb Flower Gardens   33
  Sitting Under a Favorite Tree   34
  An Early Spring Garden   36
  Spring Greeting   38
  A Candystripe Border of Spring Bulbs   39
  An Oriental Carpet   40
  Tulip Time   41
  An English Pattern Garden   42
  A Community Garden   44
  A White Border with Bulbs   45
  A Summer Bulb Garden   47
  A Fall-Blooming Bulb Garden   49

Rose Gardens   51
  A Rose Garden at the End of a Lawn   52
  A Formal Rose Garden   54

Shade Gardens   57
  A Partial Shade Garden   58
  A Woodland Shade Garden   60

Combination Gardens   63
  A Tranquil Spot   64
  A White Fragrance Garden   67
  A Salad Garden by the Kitchen Door   68
  An Herb Garden   70

Perennial Gardens   73
  A Pink and Yellow Summer Garden   74
  A Daisy Garden   76
  An Early-Blooming Perennial Garden from Seed   78
  A Garden of Perennial Everlastings   79
  An Autumn Garden for a Townhouse   81
  Ornamental Grasses   83

Container Gardens   85
  Daffodil Festival   86
  Tulip Medley   87
  Spring Harmony   89
  Flowering Herbs in a Barrel   90

A Landscaping Plan for a Quarter-Acre Plot   92

The USDA Plant Hardiness Map of the United States   94

Index   95

INTRODUCTION

The idea of collecting these small gardens in a book was developed a few years ago, to help people plan for a special area on their property. Over the years Burpee has given gardeners detailed information on how to grow vegetables and flowers. Sometimes, with all the different plants available, deciding exactly which ones to select is difficult. In the following pages we hope to help you with these decisions.

A complete garden plan takes time to work out. First, you need an accurate measurement of the area you want to plan. Next you need to decide what kind of garden you want, and where to put it. Will it be an herb garden, a plot for summer flowers, or a special flower bed next to your terrace? Will you entertain large groups or will it be a secluded refuge for two?

The design possibilities are as endless as your imagination and your interests. For instance, if you have traveled to Europe recently and came back with a statue, you might want to design a garden in typically formal fashion to include this treasure.

Pattern gardens are fun to walk through and are particularly well suited to eighteenth-century houses. The gardens of Williamsburg are elegant examples of traditional pattern gardens set gracefully beside stately homes.

Perhaps your love is houseplants and you need a place to summer them. A terrace garden can easily include shelves in a protected corner with hooks for hanging baskets. Large plants may also be rolled out and positioned in attractive groupings. Be sure to include a convenient water source so that you can wash the plants before you bring them in for the winter.

Once you have decided on the purpose of your garden, the placement will depend largely on the topography of the land around your home. Is your site in the woods or on the dunes? If so, you need to choose plants suited to that particular condition. Wherever the garden is, it should be self-contained, but also manage to relate well to its surroundings. A little garden sitting by itself in the midst of a large lawn can look very lonesome.

With the location of the garden in mind, you are ready to think about the layout. Family needs, the dimensions of the house, and the existing site conditions will be important factors in your decision. For example, if you are wondering how big to make a garden that will be adjacent to your terrace, try to decide exactly how it will be used, and how it will look in relation to the house and to the terrace itself. Confidence is easily built on a successful smaller garden.

To ensure that your garden will be attractive, certain design principles are worth considering.

Scale. Scale pertains to the size of an object relative to a human being. Good appreciation of scale can be achieved by careful consideration of the parts of a garden—is the path wide enough for two to walk side by side? Is the entrance wide enough to offer a real welcome? Is the sitting wall a comfortable height?

Proportion. The pleasing and proper relationship of one part to the whole is good proportion. To achieve this, you must again study each part so that the overall garden is at ease with all of its components.

*A pink and blue
June border features
lupines, columbines,
and coral bells.*

Unity. Unity in a composition is achieved with forms and plants of related color and texture. Don't plan a garden that is such a hodgepodge that your eye is forced to move restlessly from one plant to another.

Balance. Balance, whether symmetrical or asymmetrical, is necessary for a sense of stability. Flowers arranged evenly around a central feature, such as a grass panel, are balanced symmetrically. A garden bench that is not centered needs asymmetrical balance, created by an upright plant on one side offset by three low-growing ones on the other.

Rhythm. Rhythm in design is gained by repeating the same plant or group of plants at regular intervals in order to give a sense of continuity. You might also select plants that have the same qualities—varieties of peonies, for example—and then repeat them in rhythmical groupings with other flowers. Avoid using a large variety of plants.

Focal Point. The design of your garden should include a focal point. This might be a bench, a piece of sculpture, or a special plant. Here is where your unusual and perhaps expensive specimens count the most.

Before putting your gardening plans into action, consider just how much time you are willing to put into gardening. Scale, proportion, unity, and focal point are all important, of course, but if proper time isn't set aside for gardening, the results can be very disappointing.

In the following 40 gardens, you will find plans and ideas to add to your gardening pleasure. Just think of all the combinations—bulbs in spring, annuals and perennials in summer, and for something new, perhaps fall-blooming bulbs or roses. Don't be afraid to try your own ideas and combinations. No two gardens are ever alike—backgrounds are different, people's tastes are different. Gardens vary from year to year, and gardening is more fun if you are willing to try new things. The most important thing is to get started and learn how delightful it is to make a garden grow.

A simple, yet elegant planting of pink wax begonias and white impatiens facing an entrance.

HELPFUL HINTS

Throughout this book, we have provided plans, plant lists, and illustrations, as well as photographs of many of the plants used. Growing information is equally important. The success of your garden will depend largely upon how carefully you cater to your plants' needs. There is absolutely no way a seed can germinate without water. So, when the instructions say to water regularly, it is important to do so! Too much water can be problematic, however, particularly early in the season. Occasionally, terrific rains wash seeds away and you have to start again.

The bloom period listed here for each plant is based on planting in Zone 6; refer to the "USDA Plant Hardiness Map of the United States" (page 94) to adjust planting/bloom dates for your own zone.

In the plans that follow, each little square equals one square foot. If you decide to sketch your own plans, I would suggest doing it at ¼-inch scale. No drawing can tell you exactly where to put every seed though; at some point, you will have to rely on common sense to determine exactly how many seeds or plants you are going to need.

Orientation is important when planning your garden. North, south, east, or west—each exposure is different, and determines the amount of light that the plants will receive. Be aware of how much sun an area gets before you start to stake out your garden. Adequate drainage is equally important. Avoid a spot that tends to collect and hold water after a heavy rain. For specifics about growing annuals, perennials, and bulbs, refer to the relevant chapter introductions.

Burpee's Gardening Hot Line would be happy to answer your questions. Write or call:

W. Atlee Burpee & Company
300 Park Avenue
Warminster, PA 18974
215–674–9612
Please also write or call for a free Burpee catalog:
215–674–9633

ANNUAL FLOWER GARDENS

Annuals include a colorful group of flowers that are sown from seeds in the spring for bloom from early summer until fall. They flourish from late fall through the winter, too, in southern and Pacific Coast areas. Easy to grow and useful in so many different ways, annuals give a splash of color to beds and borders; provide a quick "garden" around a new home; fill in newly set plantings of shrubbery; add to and extend the blooming season in perennial borders; create color in bulb beds after bulbs have died down; beautify a rock garden; highlight window boxes; shade a patio or terrace; or screen out an unpleasant view. Furthermore, most annuals are prolific bloomers. Their flowers should be cut often to promote continuous bloom.

In laying out your annual garden, outline the edges, using a rope or garden hose laid on the ground. Use a spade to cut along the edges. If the area to be planted is in grass, remove the layer of sod and spade the soil to a depth of at least 6 inches. Work in compost or peat moss and rake smooth. If you fertilize in the fall, so much the better. After all danger of spring frost is past, sow the seeds according to the garden plan, carefully following the seed packet instructions for depth and spacing. Mark each variety with a label or small stake. Water with a gentle spray and keep the soil evenly moist until the seeds germinate.

Seedlings should be thinned according to the seed packet instructions. (Seedlings removed when thinning can be transplanted; set them in another garden or keep them in containers for use on a terrace.) When the plants are about 4 inches tall, cultivate lightly around them and mulch with shredded leaves, fine wood chips, or well-decayed compost. The mulch will conserve moisture and control weeds. As the flowers grow they will fill in, covering the ground. Remove dead flowers before they go to seed, in order to promote bloom. Fertilize when planting, and again in midsummer, with an all-purpose, slow-release 5–10–5 fertilizer.

An annual garden planted in the style of a classic perennial border, featuring tall cleomes in the back, snapdragons, salvias, and nicotianas in the middle, and verbenas in the front.

AN EASY, CAREFREE GARDEN

This charming, small border will provide color all summer long with easy-to-grow annuals that stand up well to hot, dry summer weather. It is designed to adapt to many places in the landscape: along a wall, fence, or hedge, or as an island in a lawn. Lengthen the garden by repeating all or part of it, or curve the outside edges and corners, maintaining approximately the same proportions. The plants require full sun, at least 6 hours per day. All may be started from seeds direct sown in the prepared ground or they can be purchased from your local garden center and planted after all danger of frost is past.

The flowers were selected because they are easy to care for, inexpensive, quick to grow from seed, and give continuous bloom throughout the summer. The nasturtiums, for example, bloom approximately 5 weeks after sowing. They will not bloom much faster if bought as "started plants," because they take time to adjust to transplanting.

Annuals will bloom more if the flowers are picked to prevent them from going to seed. Happily, this means you can reap all the benefits, enjoying cut flowers for the house as well as a long-blooming garden outside. Nasturtiums are lovely in a small vase on a side table. Both the flowers and leaves are edible and can be included in your salad—the flowers for their beauty and the leaves for their pungent, peppery flavor.

The yellow marigolds will bloom until frost, provided you remove the dead flowers. Place them on a dining room table in your favorite container and they will last a long time. I love cosmos for its airy, loose habit and use it often. Zinnias and blue cornflowers are an ideal com-

An Easy, Carefree Garden

Pour lime from a pitcher to outline your garden.

bination for an arrangement. Cleome, an old-fashioned favorite with its pungent, lemony fragrance, is showy and graceful in the garden. It is a wonderful long-lasting cut flower; when picking, carefully grasp' the central stem between the leaves to avoid the small thorns hidden at each joint. For that matter, all of the flowers can be combined in endless and varied bouquets.

OPTIONAL: For earlier bloom, all seeds with the exception of nasturtium may be started indoors; nasturtium should be sown directly in the garden. For timing and method, follow the seed packet instructions. Plant the seedlings in the prepared garden after the last frost, when the soil has warmed.

AN EASY, CAREFREE GARDEN

	COMMON NAME	VARIETY	SCIENTIFIC NAME	COLOR	HEIGHT	BLOOM	NUMBER OF SEEDLING PLANTS
A	Nasturtium	'Double Dwarf Jewel'	*Tropaeolum majus*	Mixed	1 foot	Early summer	14
B	Marigold	'Happy Days'	*Tagetes*	Yellow	10 inches	Early summer	10
C	Zinnia	'Bouquet'	*Zinnia elegans*	White	2 feet	Midsummer	12
D	Cornflower	'Blue Boy'	*Centaurea cyanus*	Blue	2½ feet	Midsummer	10
E	Cosmos	'Radiance Sensation'	*Cosmos bipinnatus*	Pink, White	4 feet	Midsummer	6
F	Cleome	'Queen'	*Cleome spinosa*	Mixed	4 feet	Midsummer	5

When planting from seed: use 1 seed packet for each variety,
except use 2 for nasturtium and 2 for cornflower.

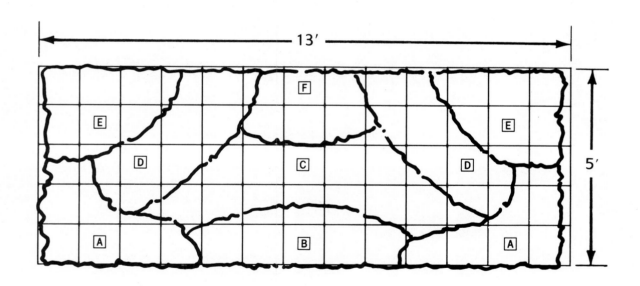

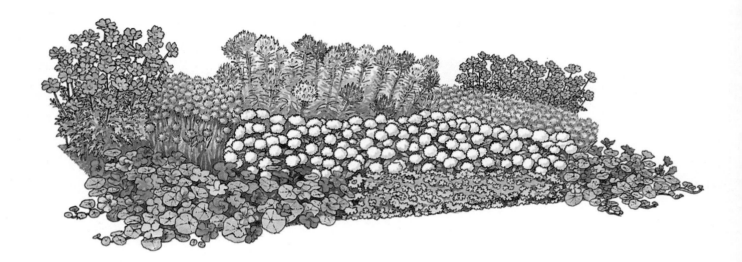

Nasturtium 'Double Dwarf Jewel'   *Marigold 'Happy Days'*   *Zinnia 'White Dasher'*

Cornflower 'Blue Boy'

*Cosmos 'Radiance
Sensation'*   *Cleome 'Queen'*

AN ISLAND OF FRAGRANCE

You will enjoy an abundance of flowers and delightful fragrance right up until frost with these easy-to-grow annuals. This garden is suitable for many places in the landscape: as an island in a sunny yard, along a south-facing wall or fence, or by a terrace. It was originally planned adjacent to a low deck so that the colors of the flowers when you looked down on them were as attractive as the fragrance.

By a terrace, the fragrance of sweet alyssum is delightful, and the plant lasts from early summer until late fall, provided it is cut back once. The mignonette has a spicy smell reminiscent of a sachet. Stock has a very sweet fragrance, especially noticeable on a warm, breezy day. *Nicotiana*, the tobacco plant, is especially nice in the evening, especially effective, therefore, near a sitting area or below a bedroom window. The annual phlox is not quite as fragrant as the perennial, but it does have a spicy scent for many weeks. Brightly colored nasturtiums are particularly pungent when picked.

For earlier bloom, you may start the phlox, *Nicotiana*, and alyssum indoors 6 to 8 weeks before outdoor planting time. For the timing and method for indoor sowing, follow the seed packet instructions. Cut back alyssum after the first bloom and it will flower prolifically all summer.

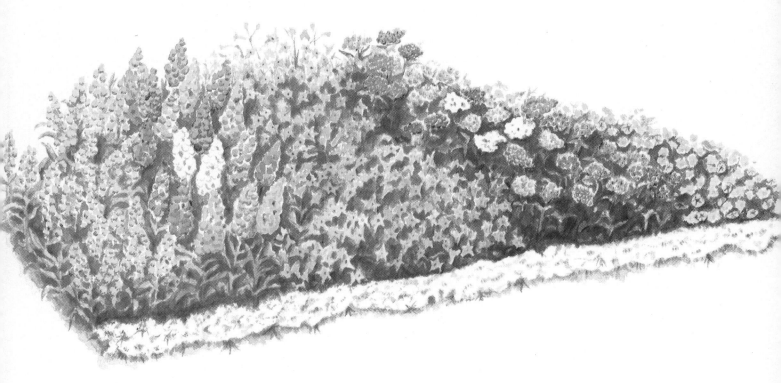

AN ISLAND OF FRAGRANCE

	COMMON NAME	VARIETY	SCIENTIFIC NAME	COLOR	HEIGHT	BLOOM	NUMBER OF SEEDLING PLANTS
A	Sweet Alyssum	'Carpet of Snow'	*Lobularia maritima*	White	1 foot	Summer to fall	Best from seed
B	Mignonette	'Grandiflora'	*Reseda odorata*	Cream	1 foot	Summer to fall	22
C	Stock	'Giant Imperial'	*Mathiola incana*	Mixed	1–1½ feet	Late spring to summer	20
D	Flowering Tobacco	'Nicki Hybrid'	*Nicotiana*	Rose	2 feet	Summer to fall	36
E	Phlox	'Fordhook Finest'	*Phlox drummondi*	Mixed	1 foot	Summer to fall	20
F	Nasturtium	'Double Dwarf Jewel'	*Tropaeolum*	Yellow	1 foot	Summer	Best from seed

When planting from seed: use 1 seed packet for each variety.

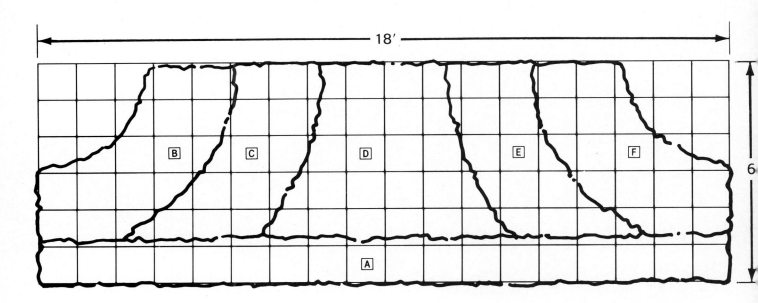

CRESCENTS OF COLOR

These little crescents were used around a lawn area where bright splashes of summer color were desired rather than a continuous flower border. I repeated the same color scheme around the edge of the grass, varying the flowers slightly in each crescent; you might choose to vary the colors instead. Perhaps you would like to use an entirely different pallette of plants: the garden might be all white, or a combination of lavenders and purples.

The crescents can be used formally or informally, alone or in groups. A single crescent could be planted in a corner near a terrace, set at the edge of a driveway, or used alongside a garden path. You can use any combination of the crescent gardens that follow to create your own design. For a larger area at the perimeter of a lawn or circular terrace, combine any 3 of these crescent gardens. Since the plants are all annuals, you can create a new plan each year. It's nice to keep photographs of each garden, so that as time passes, you can remember the combinations that you liked best.

In each case, the seeds selected are easy to grow and produce almost 12 weeks of continuous bloom. Check the information on the back of each seed packet; some varieties are best given a head start indoors.

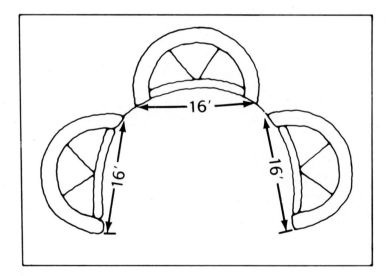

A YELLOW AND BLUE CRESCENT

This yellow and blue crescent combines complementary colors for a gay summer border. The low line of 'Happy Yellow' marigolds makes a nice sturdy edge. The triangles are filled with a long-blooming aster that will stay in bloom 4 weeks, and the delicate blue lace flower. To enjoy asters in bloom longer, you will have to plant another crop; two successive plantings will give you asters all season long. When your first crop is 4 inches high, sow new seed between the seedlings. Tall blue ageratums like 'Bavaria' would make nice alternatives to the 'Blue Lace'. Cosmos 'Bright Lights' provides airy color in the middle. The background is a yellow zinnia that I like for cutting called 'Border Beauty'.

	COMMON NAME	VARIETY	SCIENTIFIC NAME	COLOR	HEIGHT	BLOOM	NUMBER OF SEEDLING PLANTS
			A YELLOW AND BLUE CRESCENT				
A	Marigold	'Happy Yellow'	_Tagetes_	Yellow	10 inches	Summer to fall	36
B	Aster	'Burpeeana Blue Boy'	_Callistephus chinensis_	Blue	1½ feet	Summer to fall	30
C	Cosmos	'Bright Lights'	_Cosmos sulphureus_	Yellow	3 feet	Summer to fall	20
D	Blue Lace Flower		_Trachymene coerulea_	Blue	2½ feet	Summer to fall	30
E	Zinnia	'Border Beauty'	_Zinnia elegans_	Yellow	20 inches	Summer to fall	90

When planting from seed: use 1 seed packet for each variety.

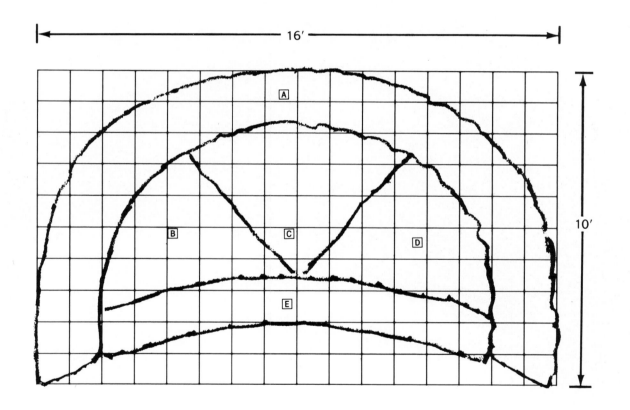

A BLUE CRESCENT

Many people love blue in the garden. This is a plan that combines a range of blues, using a mix of different flower types.

Bluebells make an excellent edging—cut them back occasionally during the summer to ensure continuous bloom until frost. The azure blue aster takes some time to develop from seed, but it is an excellent choice for cutting. Plant successively for continuous, season-long bloom. The cornflower—or bachelor's button—is one of my favorite flowers; I especially love to see them in men's lapels. Salvias have lovely spikes of brilliant blue flowers, and add immeasurably to summer bouquets.

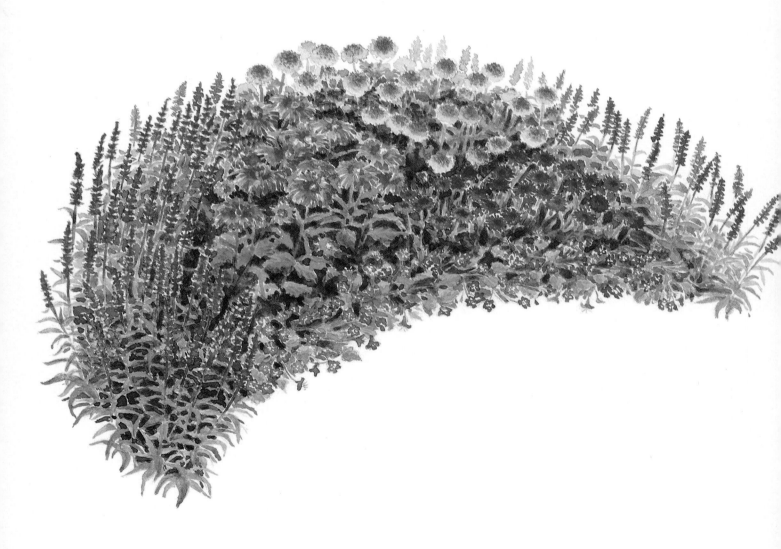

	COMMON NAME	VARIETY	SCIENTIFIC NAME	COLOR	HEIGHT	BLOOM	NUMBER OF SEEDLING PLANTS
			A BLUE CRESCENT				
A	Salvia	'Victoria'	*Salvia farinacea*	Blue	18 inches	Summer to fall	12
B	Aster	'Azure Blue'	*Callistephus chinensis*	Blue	2 feet	Summer to fall	15
C	Cornflower	'Blue Boy'	*Centaurea cyanus*	Blue	2½ feet	Summer	18
D	Cornflower	'Dwarf Blue'	*Centaurea cyanus*	Blue	1 foot	Summer	12
E	Bluebells		*Phacelia campanularia*	Violet-blue	1½ feet	Summer to fall	25

When planting from seed: use 1 seed packet for each variety.

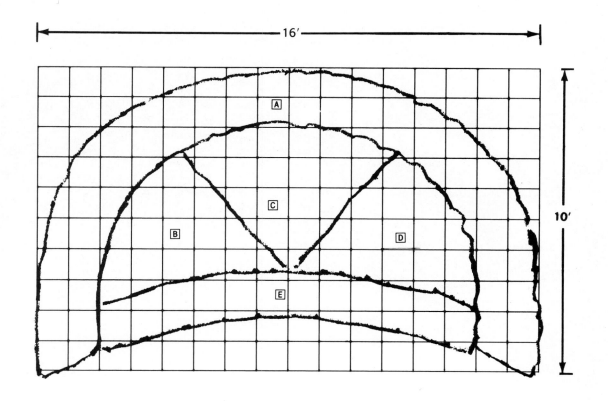

A PINK CRESCENT

I selected these pink flowers for their long season of bloom. The 'Rosie O'Day' alyssum makes an excellent edging—but be sure to cut it back and feed it in early July, so that it will continue blooming until frost.

Baby's breath adds height and airiness in the center; for continuous bloom, sow additional seed every three weeks. The asters and nicotianas are a good match for the two triangular wedges, being about the same height. Asters bloom for about 4 weeks, and if you plant another crop, you'll enjoy the season-long bloom of succession planting.

'Peter Pan Princess' zinnias surround this little crescent. If you keep picking, they will keep producing flowers until frost.

A PINK CRESCENT

	COMMON NAME	VARIETY	SCIENTIFIC NAME	COLOR	HEIGHT	BLOOM	NUMBER OF SEEDLING PLANTS
A	Alyssum	'Rosie O'Day'	*Lobularia maritima*	Pink	6 inches	Summer to fall	15
B	Aster	'Burpeeana Rose'	*Callistephus chinensis*	Pink	1½ feet	Summer to fall	12
C	Baby's Breath	'Covent Garden White'	*Gypsophila elegans*	White	1½ feet	Summer to fall	9
D	Flowering Tobacco	'Domino'	*Nicotiana alata*	Pink with white	1½ feet	Summer to fall	12
E	Zinnia	'Peter Pan Princess'	*Zinnia elegans*	Pink	2½ feet	Summer to fall	24

When planting from seed: use 1 seed packet for each variety.

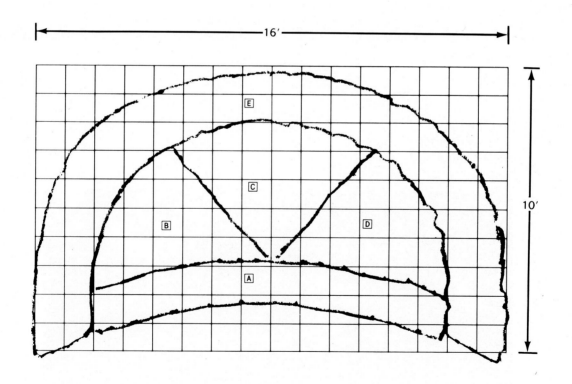

A CUTTING GARDEN

A cutting garden is a joy all summer, for it gives you enough flowers to cut for yourself and to give away to friends. It's fun to go out and pick a handful of flowers, then do an arrangement in a lovely, old-fashioned bowl. A mixture of fragrant *dianthus* would be delightful on a table near your favorite chair, for example. An old sugar bowl filled with marigolds and set on the kitchen table would also be a pleasant sight. Imagine cosmos, which is light and airy, in a pair of tall, blue vases on a mantlepiece. In an extra bedroom, a combination of annual baby's breath and zinnias is a welcome sight for entering guests.

These are the pleasures that a cutting garden provides; but to start, you have to think about where your flowers are going to grow. A cutting garden would sit nicely against a south-facing wall or fence. If it is close to a hedge, be sure to provide a path between the hedge and the garden border. This garden might be planted close to—or even in—a terrace. The location you choose must have sun at least 6 hours a day. The narrow paths in the garden itself can be grass, pine needles, or gravel.

All of the annuals in this garden are prolific bloomers and should be cut often to promote flowering. To prevent wilting, cut only early or late in the day. In very warm weather, take along a bucket of water and put the flowers in it as soon as they are cut. Let the flowers stand in water for several hours before recutting the stems and arranging them. Remove all leaves that would be below the waterline. For long-lasting arrangements, you might consider adding sugar and bleach (1 teaspoon each per quart of water). Bleach keeps fungus from growing, and the sugar feeds the flowers.

For season-long bloom, make successive plantings of the asters and baby's breath.

*The abundant
end-of-summer harvest
from A Cutting
Garden*

	COMMON NAME	VARIETY	SCIENTIFIC NAME	COLOR	HEIGHT	BLOOM	NUMBER OF SEEDLING PLANTS
			A CUTTING GARDEN				
A	Baby's Breath	'Covent Garden White'	*Gypsophila elegans*	White	1½ feet	Summer to fall	6
B	Blue Lace Flower		*Trachymene caerulea*	Blue	2½ feet	Summer	18
C	Pinks	'Double Gaiety'	*Dianthus*	Mixed	1 foot	Summer to fall	18
D	Aster	'Burpeeana Extra Early'	*Callistephus chinensis*	Mixed	1½ feet	Summer to fall	18
E	Pincushion Flower	'Giant Imperial'	*Scabiosa*	Mixed	3 feet	Summer to fall	10
F	Marigold	'Sweet 'n Yellow'	*Tagetes*	Yellow	2 feet	Summer to fall	5
G	Cosmos	'Bright Lights'	*Cosmos sulphureus*	Mixed	3 feet	Summer to fall	5
H	Zinnia	'Giant Flower'	*Zinnia elegans*	Mixed	2½ feet	Summer to fall	10
I	Cosmos	'Sensation'	*Cosmos bipinnatus*	Mixed	4 feet	Summer to fall	16

When planting from seed: use 1 seed packet for each variety.

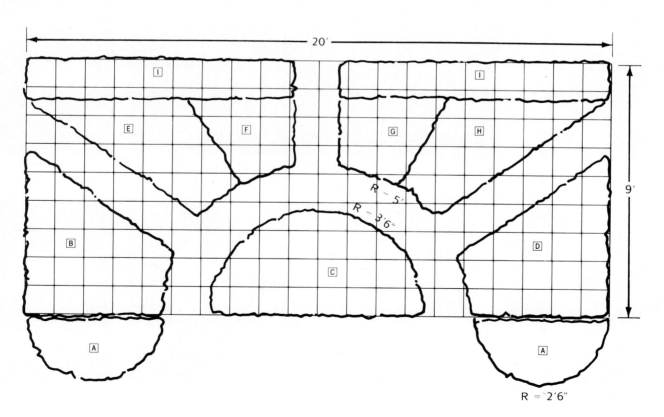

Baby's breath 'Covent Garden White'

Blue lace flower

Pinks 'Double Gaiety'

Aster 'Burpeeanna Extra Early'

Pincushion flower 'Giant Imperial'

Marigold 'Sweet 'n Yellow'

Cosmos 'Bright Lights'

Zinnia 'Giant Flower'

Cosmos 'Sensation'

A GARDEN OF ANNUAL EVERLASTINGS

This garden is easy to grow and will be attractive all summer long, providing an abundance of flowers for cutting and drying. It has been designed for any corner location that receives full sun.

All of these flowers are easy to dry and will provide a handsome variety of material for long-lasting arrangements. Some of these everlastings—strawflower, globe amaranth, immortelle, statice, and bells of Ireland—are dried for their flowers; starflower and love-in-a-mist are dried for their handsome seed pods. (The flowers of love-in-a-mist can be dried, but it is necessary to use a commercial flower-drying product.) Gather the flowers before the full peak of bloom. If you leave flowers outside after bloom, rain and wind will mar their beauty. Cut these flowers in the heat of the day. Strip all foliage from the stems, tie in small bunches by the ends of the stems and hang to dry in a dark, well-ventilated place for 2–3 weeks. Colors will hold best if the flowers are kept out of direct sunlight. Flowers will feel crisp when dry.

These varieties were selected for their unusual qualities, both as summer-blooming plants and as a source for winter bouquets. (Starflower seed pods can even be used for Christmas tree ornaments if brightly spray-painted.) With such a collection you can make your own Christmas bouquets at very little expense. Just dry as above, arrange the flowers in an unusual container—a sugar bowl, a wine glass—and you will have a lovely gift for the holidays.

A GARDEN OF ANNUAL EVERLASTINGS

	COMMON NAME	VARIETY	SCIENTIFIC NAME	COLOR	HEIGHT	BLOOM	NUMBER OF SEEDLING PLANTS
A	Strawflower	Dwarf	*Helichrysum*	Mixed	1½ feet	Summer to fall	7
B	Love-in-a-Mist	'Persian Jewels'	*Nigella damascena*	Mixed	1–1½ feet	Summer	12
C	Globe Amaranth	Mixed	*Gomphrena globosa*	Mixed	15–20 inches	Summer to fall	5
D	Immortelle	Mixed	*Xeranthemum annuum*	Mixed	2 feet	Summer	7
E	Starflower		*Scabiosa stellata*	Light brown	2 feet	Summer to fall	9
F	Statice	'Art Shades'	*Limonium sinuata*	Rose	2 feet	Summer	6
G	Bells of Ireland		*Molucella laevis*	Green	2½ feet	Summer	9

When planting from seed: use 1 seed packet for each variety.

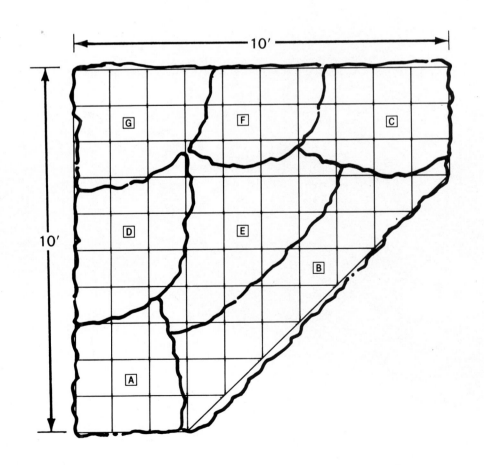

A RAINBOW OF IMPATIENS

This little border of variously colored impatiens would be lovely along a pathway leading to some special place in your garden. It was originally planned to go beneath a crabapple alley connecting the back door to a sitting garden. In the springtime the alley is a canopy of crabapple blossoms, and then in summer the impatiens take over, lining the path with banks of flowers.

Impatiens are spectacular performers all season long. They provide color for those partially shaded portions of the garden where color is so difficult to achieve. The large blossoms are now available as both singles and doubles, and the flower production is enormous. They're carefree plants too—they need no pinching to maintain their neat habit. Impatiens are a fine choice for shaded patio containers, also. They are particularly striking combined with caladiums.

They last well into the fall, and can even be transferred indoors once frost arrives. Cuttings taken in late summer become lovely pot plants in a bright winter window.

If your spot is sunny, you might try using the newer 'New Guinea' impatiens that tolerate more heat and sun than the traditional shade-loving varieties.

These impatiens are all from Burpee's Dazzler Series. They stand about 8 inches high, and will bloom all season.

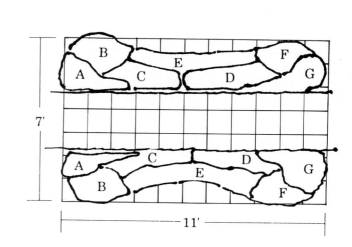

A Rainbow of Impatiens was repeated many times to completely cover the length of this allée.

A RAINBOW OF IMPATIENS		
IMPATIENS		**NUMBER OF SEEDLING PLANTS**
A	Blush	18
B	Coral	12
C	Rose	12
D	Violet	12
E	White with pink eye	18
F	Red	12
G	Pink	18

MARIGOLDS BY THE BACK DOOR

Here's a sunny collection of marigolds to provide a welcoming splash of color at either side of an entranceway. These facing beds couldn't be easier to grow and maintain—all the seeds can be direct sown where they are to grow and will flower in about 6 weeks. Choose a location with good drainage that receives at least 6 hours of sunlight a day.

Marigolds come in many different sizes and shapes and, given a sunny spot, they all thrive on benign neglect. All of them tolerate heat and drought remarkably well, resist disease, and come as close to being carefree as any flower available. Their pungent fragrance makes them a natural insect repellent; marigolds are known as a companion plant for tomatoes because they are said to discourage nematodes. Any of the marigolds are handsome in a vegetable garden as well, particularly when used as a low edging.

How cheerful to have a mass of bright yellow and orange flowers blooming outside your back door to enjoy every day. Because of their long season of bloom, marigolds have always been one of my favorite flowers.

	COMMON NAME	VARIETY	SCIENTIFIC NAME	COLOR	HEIGHT	BLOOM
A	Marigold	'Golden Climax'	*Tagetes*	Deep golden yellow	3 feet	All summer
B	Marigold	'First Lady'	*Tagetes*	Light yellow	1½ feet	All summer
C	Marigold	'Snowdrift'	*Tagetes*	White	1½ to 2 feet	All summer
D	Marigold	'Naughty Marietta'	*Tagetes*	Golden yellow with maroon	1 foot	All summer
E	Marigold	'Pygmy Primrose'	*Tagetes*	Yellow	7 inches	All summer

MARIGOLDS BY THE BACK DOOR (table title)

When planting from seed: Use 1 seed packet for each variety, except use 2 packets for First Lady.

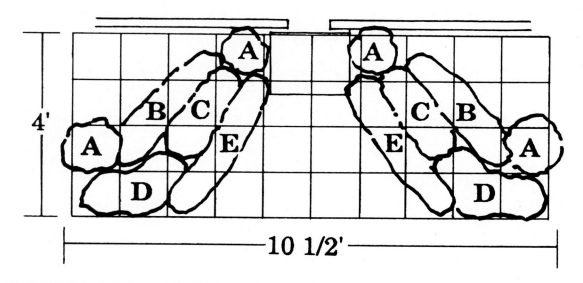

A portion of the design Marigolds by the Back Door

BULB FLOWER GARDENS

Of all forms of gardening, planting hardy bulbs is among the easiest and perhaps the most satisfying. Select a location that is well-drained and receives at least 4 hours of sun each day. Lay out the general outline of the garden, using a rope or garden hose. Use a spade to cut along the edge. Dig up the garden area within the boundaries you've cut, spading down to about 12 inches. Add compost or peat moss to the area and work it in. You may apply Holland Bulb Booster℠ to the top of the soil in the fall; this slow-release fertilizer will nourish your plants over the entire growing season. If the soil is very dry, water well before planting. I like to soak my daffodils in water, too, for ½ hour before planting; this helps them root more quickly. Prepare the bed a few weeks before planting, if possible, so it will settle and be ready for the bulbs when you plant them; if you can't prepare the bed early, just add soil if needed when the garden has settled to level it.

Plant the bulbs as soon as you receive them. Planting depth varies, but the simple rule of thumb I use is that the depth should be about three times the height of the bulb. I think bulbs look best planted in clumps of similar varieties rather than rows. Set them close together and water well. After blooming, remove faded flowers, fertilize, and keep well-watered. Do not remove the foliage until it dies down naturally. (This is the time when the leaves are producing buds for next year's flowers.)

Certain bulbs, like tulips and hyacinths, have to be replaced every year or two. Longevity really depends on growing conditions. If you can provide the ideal conditions—sun, good drainage and circulation of air, and food—flowers will continue to set inside the bulbs.

Bulbs supply much of the garden's spring color. From the earliest snowdrops and crocuses, they provide a steady parade lasting into the summer, when the hardy lilies bloom, and on into fall, with autumn crocuses. Many of the early-blooming bulbs flower and fade before trees and shrubs have fully leafed out; thus you can plant them in areas which will later be shaded. Bloom periods for bulbs are usually described as early, mid, or late season. Where you live and the weather, as always, will dictate on what dates you can expect your bulbs to come up.

Bulbs may be used in formal beds, in groups by a doorway, in front of foundation plantings, beneath shrubs, and under trees. Many lend themselves to naturalizing—planting in large informal drifts, as if Nature had set them there. The easiest way to do this without creating a contrived look is to toss the bulbs by the handful and plant them where they land. Bulbs are permanent investments in beauty: snowdrops, crocuses, and daffodils are just a few of the bulbs that will actually increase in number and loveliness with the years.

By planning bloom time, a steady parade of color can march through your garden. Here, planted in large informal drifts, late-blooming daffodils bloom with early tulips and hyacinths.

A SITTING GARDEN UNDER A FAVORITE TREE

This garden reminds me of an old Japanese maple I played under when I was a child. Every spring we looked forward to the daffodils coming up—what varieties, I don't know, but we always picked a few to take in to our mother. I selected these varieties of daffodil because they are strong, sturdy types—tried and true.

Choose a partially shady site under a tree (but not too near the trunk of the tree where root growth is heaviest). Set bulbs as indicated on the plan, at the depth and spacing recommended on the packages. Set vinca as indicated in the planting instructions, throughout the areas where you've already set your bulbs. Water well, and fertilize both bulbs and vinca.

During the garden's first year, you may want to plant some colorful annuals between the young vincas. Impatiens, ageratum, coleus, and the fibrous-rooted begonia are a few that will grow well in partial shade. Mulch around the plants to control weeds and conserve soil moisture. With simple care, both daffodils and vinca will fill in and become more beautiful each year.

'Cantatrice' has pure white petals and a narrow, lemon yellow trumpet that matures to white.

'King Alfred' is a very old favorite, large-trumpeted with a strong yellow color. There are some new varieties that are equally lovely.

'Ice Follies' has very large, showy flowers with fresh white petals and a shallow fluted cup of pale yellow that changes to off-white and lasts well.

Vinca minor is the groundcover that I prefer to use with daffodils. It is shallow-rooted and has lovely blue flowers.

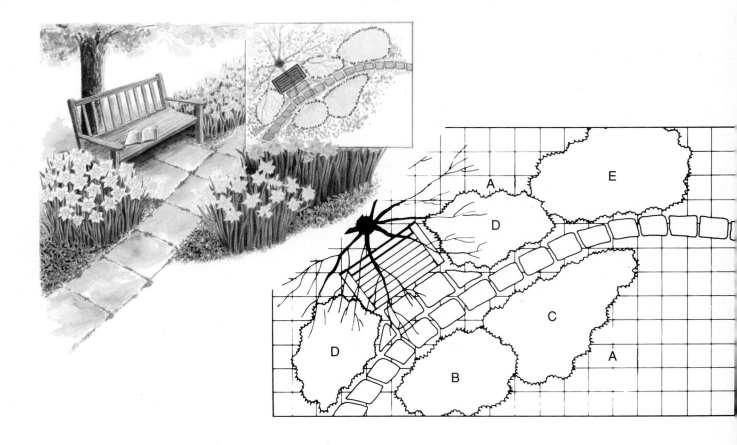

A SITTING GARDEN UNDER A FAVORITE TREE

	COMMON NAME	VARIETY	SCIENTIFIC NAME	COLOR	HEIGHT	BLOOM	NUMBER OF PLANTS
A	Vinca		*Vinca minor*	Lavender blue	2–4 inches	Early spring	100
B	Daffodil	'Cantatrice'	*Narcissus*	White with light lemon	1 foot	March–April	16
C	Daffodil	'King Alfred'	*Narcissus*	Golden yellow	1½ feet	March–April	32
D	Daffodil	'Ice Follies'	*Narcissus*	White with primrose yellow	1–1½ feet	April	48
E	Daffodil	'St. Patrick's Day'	*Narcissus*	Soft and light yellow	1–1½ feet	April	72

Vinca

Daffodil 'Cantatrice'

Daffodil 'Ice Follies'

Daffodil 'St. Patrick's Day'

Daffodil 'King Alfred'

AN EARLY SPRING GARDEN

This tiny garden was designed to be planted outside of a bay window, where it could easily be seen from indoors, but it will do just as beautifully in any sunny location along an outside wall. It blooms in sequence, so don't be surprised when all the plants don't come up at once. They will bloom in this order:

Winter aconite has yellow, buttercuplike flowers with green, frilled collars that bloom in late February or early March. Aconite increases rapidly by both seed and division, and it thrives in the partial shade of deciduous trees. Optional: Soak very dry tubers in water for 24 hours before planting, to plump them and give them a head start in putting down roots.

Snowdrops are a welcome sight in earliest spring, with charming flowers that barely wait for the snow to disappear. Snowdrops are pretty naturalized with winter aconite under trees and shrubs, and will form dense colonies if left undisturbed.

Anemone produces masses of starry, daisy-like flowers. If grown in partial shade and rich soil, it will bloom longer than any other spring flower. With its attractive ferny foliage, this *anemone* spreads freely and makes a lovely sight planted in drifts.

'Snow' crocuses are often seen poking their little cups up through the snow, providing the first real flush of spring color. In the South, they will bloom in January; in the North, they will wait until February or March. They are noteworthy for their unusual color blends (not found in the larger hybrids) and profuse bloom—several flowers per bulb is not unusual. Plant in large numbers to create a good display. They are especially effective naturalized in grass, under deciduous shrubs or trees, or in the rock garden. For earliest bloom, plant them in a sheltered, sunny location.

The iris is a charming plant and one of the first spring bulbs to bloom. It naturalizes well and is ideal for rock gardens, at the front of the border, or clustered in foundation plantings.

Puschkinia has dense clusters of dainty, soft blue flowers with dark blue stripes that bloom in early spring. It does well in sun or part shade, under deciduous trees and shrubs, and is a fine rock garden plant.

AN EARLY SPRING GARDEN

	COMMON NAME	VARIETY	SCIENTIFIC NAME	COLOR	HEIGHT	BLOOM	NUMBER OF BULBS
A	Crocus	'Snow Crocus Mixture'	*Crocus chrysanthus*	Mixed	3–4 inches	February–March	48
B	Snowdrops		*Galanthus nivalis*	White	3–4 inches	February–March	72
C	Winter Aconite		*Eranthis hyemalis*	Yellow	3–4 inches	Early March	96
D	Windflower	'Pink Star'	*Anemone blanda*	Pink	3–6 inches	Early March	72
E	Windflower	'White Splendor'	*Anemone blanda*	White	3–6 inches	Early March	72
F	Dwarf Iris		*Iris reticulata*	Mixed	4–6 inches	Late March–early April	24
G	Glory of the Snow		*Chionodixa gigantea*	Blue	4–6 inches	Late March–early April	144
H	Puschkinia		*Puschkinia libanotica*	Blue	4–6 inches	Late March–early April	36

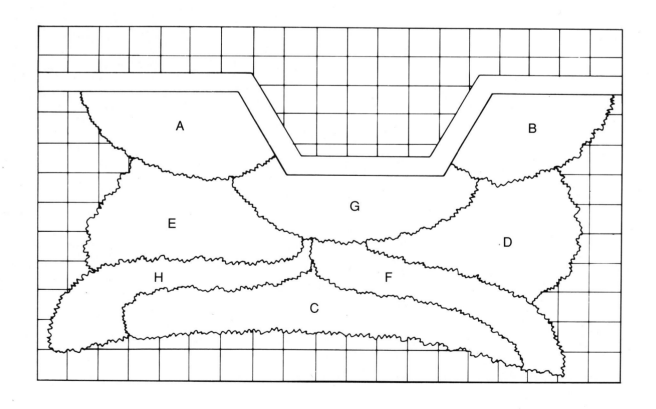

SPRING GREETING

This daffodil garden is designed as a cheerful welcome to be planted along the walkway to an entrance, front or rear. It includes a combination of varying heights and flower shapes, in shades of yellow and white, and will bloom for approximately 6 weeks: late March through the end of April. Plant this garden where you will see and enjoy it often; if you have a back door that leads to a clothesline, try planting these daffodils for a magical spring lift. When the daffodil leaves have died down (which is often not until June), try overplanting with the mixture of marigolds featured in "Marigolds by the Back Door."

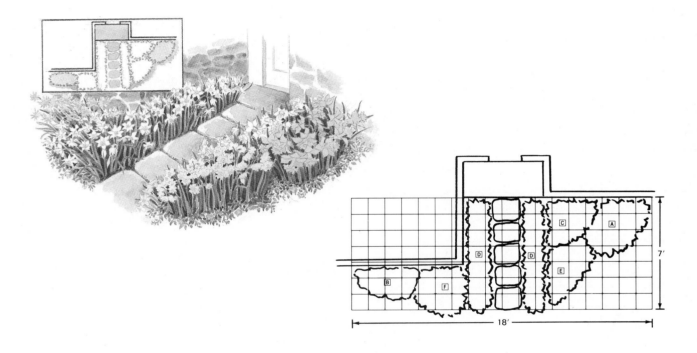

			SPRING GREETING				
	COMMON NAME	**VARIETY**	**SCIENTIFIC NAME**	**COLOR**	**HEIGHT**	**BLOOM**	**NUMBER OF BULBS**
A	Daffodil	'King Alfred'	*Narcissus*	Golden yellow	1½ feet	March–April	8
B	Daffodil	'Rip Van Winkle'	*Narcissus*	Light yellow with gold center	8 inches	April	16
C	Daffodil	'White Lion'	*Narcissus*	Soft white with yellow center	18 inches	April	8
D	Daffodil	'Silver Chimes'	*Narcissus*	White petals with pale yellow cups	15 inches	April	32
E	Daffodil	'Cheerfulness'	*Narcissus*	Creamy white	1½ feet	Mid–late April	16
F	Daffodil	'Thalia'	*Narcissus*	White	12–15 inches	Mid–late April	16

A CANDYSTRIPE BORDER OF SPRING BULBS

This enchanting garden provides a splash of color for 6 weeks, from early to late spring. The bulbs bloom in an overlapping sequence, beginning with the windflower and ending with tulips— the lily-flowered 'White Triumphator' and the single late 'Cordell Hull'. The garden would work well between a driveway and the side of a building, fence, or wall. It can also be used along the edge of a walk or terrace. Any narrow strip that receives 4 to 6 hours of full sun each day is an appropriate place for bulbs. If purchased by mail, they will be shipped to you at the proper planting time in the fall; plant them as soon as possible.

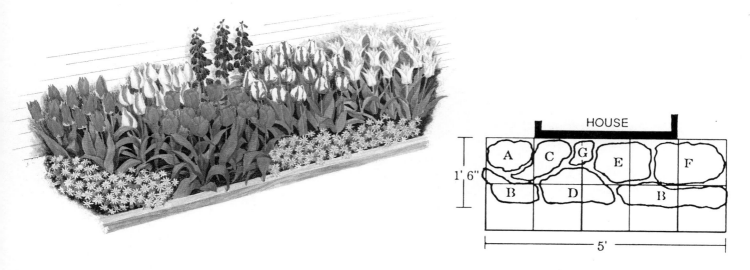

	COMMON NAME	VARIETY	SCIENTIFIC NAME	COLOR	HEIGHT	BLOOM	NUMBER OF BULBS
A	Tulip	'Red Emperor'	*Tulipa*	Scarlet with black	1½ feet	Early	12
B	Windflower	'White Splendor'	*Anemone blanda*	White with yellow	3–6 inches	Early March	36
C	Tulip	'Garden Party'	*Tulipa*	White with rose	1½ feet	Mid-season	12
D	Tulip	'Parade'	*Tulipa*	Red with black	2 feet	Late mid-season	12
E	Tulip	'Cordell Hull'	*Tulipa*	Deep red with white	2 feet	Late season	18
F	Tulip	'White Triumphator'	*Tulipa*	Snow white	2 feet	Late	18
G	Fritillaria	'Adiyaman'	*Fritillaria persica*	Chocolaty purple	2½ feet	Early–mid tulip season	3

A CANDYSTRIPE BORDER OF SPRING BULBS

AN ORIENTAL CARPET

In a spot that is very visible, try planting some of the early spring bulbs. These little bulbs are inexpensive and easy to plant, and each year they will increase and give weeks of pleasure. They should be planted early, because they can dry out quickly. I like to use them in masses of at least 25 bulbs each for the best effect.

White snowdrops bloom as the snow disappears, sometimes in February. Plant them close together —3 inches apart seems best—and even in the shade they will come up and return each year.

The grape hyacinths are enchanting, with fresh blue flowers that seed freely; in time, you have masses of welcome newcomers.

The *Tulipa tarda* will produce clusters of 3- to 6-inch bright yellow and white star-shaped flowers that bloom for a long time. The bulbs are long-lived as well.

Since all of these bulbs bloom early, you might fill the beds with a groundcover—*Ajuga, Nepeta, Plumbago,* or *Euonymus,* for example. A combination of two groundcovers can be unusually lovely.

Grape hyacinth 'Blue Spike'

Species tulip

Snowdrop

		AN ORIENTAL CARPET			
	Common Name	**Scientific Name**	**Height**	**Bloom**	**Number of Bulbs**
A	Snowdrop	*Galanthus nivalis*	3–4 inches	Early spring	6–8
B	Grape hyacinth	*Muscari armeniacum*	6 inches	Early spring	6–8
C	Species tulip	*Tulipa tarda*	3 inches	Mid April	6–8

TULIP TIME

This garden of tulips and wood hyacinths is designed to be planted against a building wall or a background of evergreen shrubbery, but it could also be adapted to the edge of a terrace. The tulip varieties have been combined to provide a succession of bloom for approximately 4 to 6 weeks.

The edging of wood hyacinths comes up fairly early and blooms late with a lovely, blue nodding flower which lasts a long time. The large-flowered 'Pink and White Emperors' come out in April. 'Garden Party' follows, producing white blooms with dramatic deep pink along the petal edges. 'Sweet Harmony' is an old favorite of mine. It comes late, with pale yellow to creamy white blooms, flowing with 'Maytime' for a brilliant finale to the tulip season.

'Maytime' has urn-shaped, lily-flowered blooms and gracefully reflexing petals, making it among the most refined tulips. The intense rose-violet petals are edged with white.

After tulips have finished blooming, plant annuals between them for continuous summer bloom.

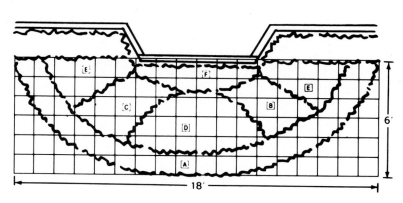

	COMMON NAME	VARIETY	SCIENTIFIC NAME	COLOR	HEIGHT	BLOOM	NUMBER OF BULBS
A	Wood Hyacinth	'Blue Excelsior'	*Scilla campanulata*	Blue	1½ feet	Late May	72
B	Tulip	'Pink Emperor'	*Tulipa fosteriana*	Rose with yellow	1½ feet	Early season (early April)	12
C	Tulip	'White Emperor'	*Tulipa fosteriana*	White	1½ feet	Early season (early April)	12
D	Tulip	'Garden Party'	*Tulipa triumph*	White with pink	18 inches	Late mid-season (early May)	24
E	Tulip	'Sweet Harmony'	*Tulipa single*	Pale lemon yellow and white	2–2½ feet	Late season (mid–late May)	24
F	Tulip	'Maytime'	*Tulipa lily-flowered*	Rose-violet edged with white	22–26 inches	Late season (May)	24

TULIP TIME

AN ENGLISH PATTERN GARDEN

This pattern garden fits neatly into a 20-foot square. It features a central sundial or sculpture. The bulbs are massed in small beds, which are a joy to walk around. Such a formal plan needs to be contained with a strong edge. As an alternative to the 'Gold Drop', I might suggest a holly hedge or a low wall. The paths can be grass, brick, or flagstone, edged with brick to accent the pattern of the beds.

When the bulbs have died down these little beds can be filled with annuals. Imagine an all-grey annual garden, or a combination of everlastings that will be colorful from July until frost.

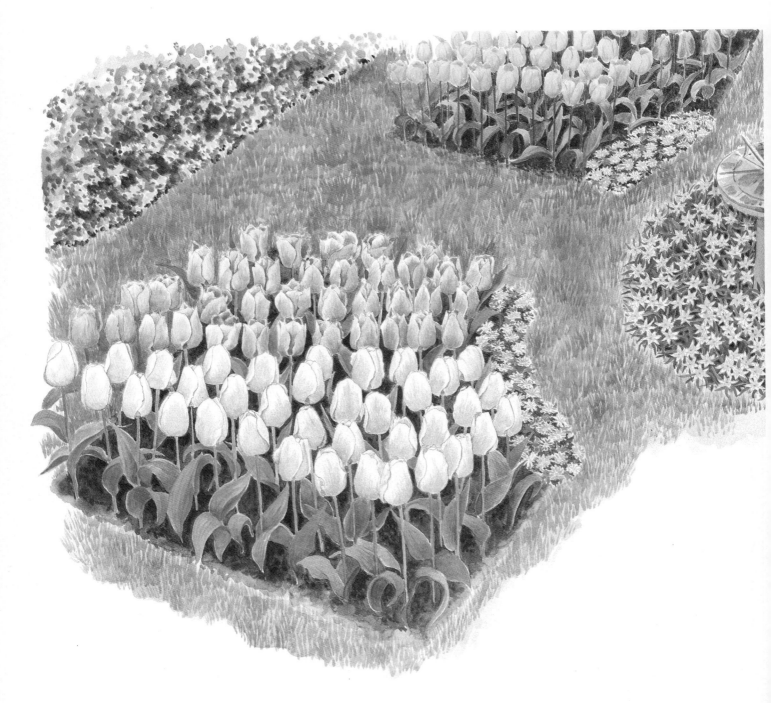

	COMMON NAME	VARIETY	SCIENTIFIC NAME	COLOR	HEIGHT	BLOOM	NUMBER OF BULBS
A	Windflower		*Anemone blanda*	Mixed	3–6 inches	Early March	240
B	Tulip	'Tarda'	*Tulipa dasystemon*	Yellow and white	3 inches	Mid April	72
C	Tulip	'Elizabeth Arden'	*Tulipa Darwin Hybrid*	Pink	2 feet	Late April–early May	36
D	Tulip	'Golden Parade'	*Tulipa Darwin Hybrid*	Yellow with black	2 feet	Late April–early May	36
E	Tulip	'Beauty of Appeldorn'	*Tulipa Darwin Hybrid*	Yellow with red	2 feet	Late April–May	36
F	Tulip	'Ivory Floradale'	*Tulipa Darwin Hybrid*	Cream	2 feet	Late April–May	72
G	Tulip	'Apricot Beauty'	*Tulipa Single Early*	Apricot	1–1½ feet	Late April–May	36
H	Tulip	'White Dream'	*Tulipa Triumph*	Ivory	2 feet	May	36
I	Tulip	'Shirley'	*Tulipa Single Late*	Ivory	2 feet	May	36
J	Potentilla	'Gold Drop'	*Potentilla fruticosa*	Yellow	12–15 inches	June–September	40

AN ENGLISH PATTERN GARDEN

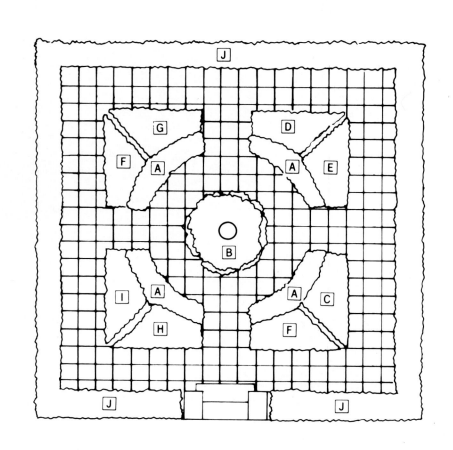

A COMMUNITY GARDEN

This garden is designed to be planted around the base of a flagpole, but it could be altered to accent any special feature. You can change the shape of the planting area, making it square, oval, or rectangular. Or, plant the bulbs in a circle without a central focal point.

The garden design reflects the mature size of the plants, allowing room for growth. Plant the bulbs when they are received or as soon after that as possible. Tulips and hyacinths usually do not bloom well after the first year. For the best display each spring, pull out the bulbs after they've bloomed and plant them in cutting gardens or elsewhere; only a portion of them will bloom again the second year. Replant the area with red geraniums, blue salvia, and an edging of white alyssum to continue the patriotic theme. Mulch around the plants to control weeds and conserve soil moisture. In the fall, remove the annuals and replant with new tulip and hyacinth bulbs.

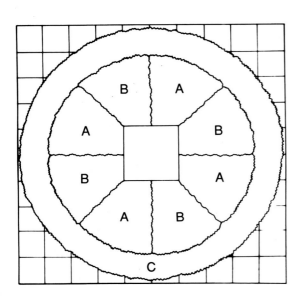

	COMMON NAME	VARIETY	SCIENTIFIC NAME	COLOR	HEIGHT (inches)	BLOOM	NUMBER OF BULBS
A	Tulip	'Red Emperor'	*Tulipa fosteriana*	Scarlet with black base	18	April	144
B	Tulip	'White Emperor'	*Tulipa fosteriana*	White	18	April	144
C	Hyacinth	'Dutch Blue'	*Hyacinth orientalis*	Delft blue	10	April	96

A COMMUNITY GARDEN

A WHITE BORDER WITH BULBS

This garden of white bulbs is designed to be planted in front of an evergreen hedge. The white flowers show up well against a dark green background. They are stunning in the daytime and very romantic at night, reflecting the moonlight. The daffodils and hyacinths are fragrant, creating a very special spot that is lovely day and night.

The 'Snowstorm' crocus will be the first to bloom. This is a large-flowered variety. It opens and closes according to the temperature.

Then comes 'Thalia', with its graceful, small flowers and exquisite perfume. It is lovely in the garden and good for picking as well.

'Mt. Hood' has large, white petals and a pale yellow trumpet that matures to snowy white. It is tall, growing to 18 inches. The hyacinth 'L'Innocence' is a pure white that is very fragrant and more upright and sturdy than other hyacinths. Tulip 'White Dream' has yellow anthers.

To provide bloom all season, you may want to plant some annuals after the bulbs have finished flowering. Try white-flowering lilies, gladiolus, and callas. Silver- or white-foliaged plants such as dusty miller and caladiums would complement the flowers nicely.

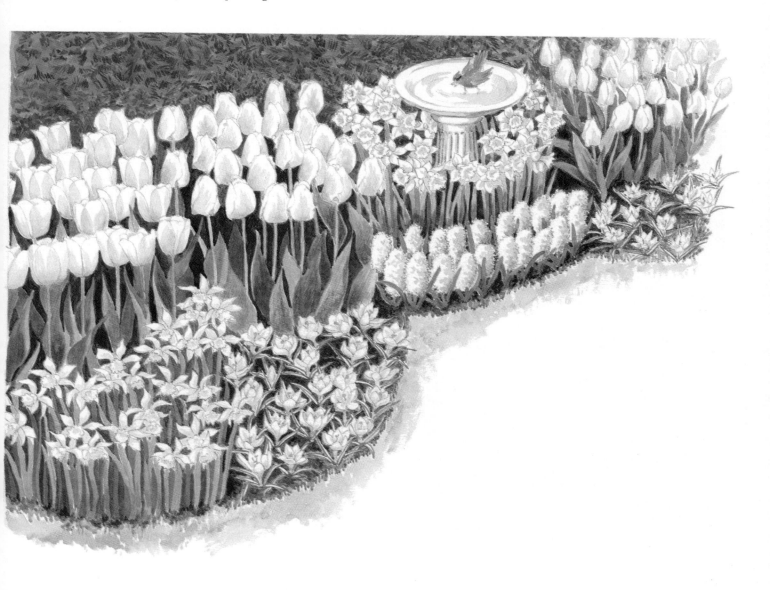

A WHITE BORDER WITH BULBS

	COMMON NAME	VARIETY	SCIENTIFIC NAME	COLOR	HEIGHT	BLOOM	NUMBER OF PLANTS
A	Crocus	'Snowstorm'	*Crocus*	Pure white	3–4 inches	March	24
B	Daffodil	'Mount Hood'	*Narcissus*	White and pale yellow	1½ feet	April	24
C	Daffodil	'Thalia'	*Narcissus*	White	12–15 inches	Late mid-season	24
D	Hyacinth	'Innocence'	*Hyacinthus orientalis*	Pure white	10 inches	April	12
E	Tulip	'Ivory Floradale'	*Tulipa Darwin Hybrid*	Creamy white, sometimes flecked with red	2 feet	Late mid-season	24
F	Tulip	'White Dream'	*Tulipa Triumph*	Ivory with yellow	2 feet	Mid-season (Late April–early May)	36

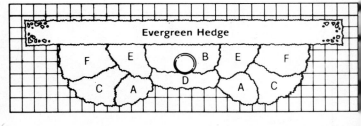

An all-white garden reflects the moonlight. Harmony is achieved in this garden by massing and repeating bleeding hearts, tulips, and candytuft.

A SUMMER BULB GARDEN

This summer bulb garden was designed to provide a long season of bloom. It could be planted against a fence, where it would be protected from the wind and require minimal staking. Remember that some of these bulbs have to be taken up in the fall. Lilies, *Liriope*, and *Lycoris* are hardy and can stay in the ground.

Lycoris squamigera, hardy amaryllis, has handsome, star-shaped leaves that appear in early spring, and then vanish in early summer. In late summer, 2- to 3-foot flower stems spring up as if by magic—thus the alternate common name 'Magic Lily'.

The clusters of pink, lilylike flowers are sweetly fragrant. Place a stake to mark where bulbs have been planted, so they are not cultivated or dug up.

Caladium, 'Candidum' is the most popular caladium for shady or semishady areas in a summer garden. It is an elegant foliage plant with white leaves and green veins. Caladiums are suitable for beds or containers, and can be kept as houseplants as well.

Dahlia, 'Bonnie Esperance' is a low-growing plant, ideally suited for edging. It thrives without staking, producing soft pink blooms on compact bushes.

Butterfly gladiolus are midway between the miniature and the standard glads known to all. These plants are exceptionally strong, and need no staking. Grouped in the garden, they provide a marvelous jack-in-the-box effect. Each floret combines two or more colors, giving the plant a far less formal and more graceful look than their bigger cousins. Use butterfly gladiolus toward the back of the border.

Lilium, 'Connecticut Beauty' is a compact early bloomer, with huge flowers of shimmering yellow. Unusually attractive foliage clothes the 3-foot plants that bloom from late June through early July.

The tuberose, 'Excelsior' is an old-fashioned, exceptionally fragrant flower that is lovely for cutting. The double, waxy white flowers are set closely on 2- to 3-foot spikes. Tuberoses bloom late summer into fall, but they are not hardy.

Liriope, 'Big Blue' has arching tufts of grass-like, evergreen foliage. It is excellent as a groundcover or as an edging plant. Clusters of lavender flowers appear in late summer and are followed by spikes of lavender-blue berries. *Liriope* is easy to grow. For clean-looking foliage, I suggest cutting plants back in early spring, before the new growth starts.

Lift the bulbs that aren't hardy after the first heavy frost has turned their leaves brown. Store them in peat moss or dry sand in a cool place. You can start them indoors in early spring, or set them outside once the ground has warmed up completely.

Caladium 'Candidum'

Hardy amaryllis

Tuberose 'Excel
Dwarf Pearl'

Lily 'Connecticut Beauty'

Butterfly gladiolus, mixed colors

Lily turf 'Big Blue'

Dahlia 'Bonnie Esperand

A SUMMER BULB GARDEN

	COMMON NAME	VARIETY	SCIENTIFIC NAME	COLOR	HEIGHT	BLOOM	NUMBER OF BULBS
A	Hardy Amaryllis		Lycoris squamigera	Lavender-pink	2–3 feet	Late summer	15
B	Caladium	'Candidum'	Caladium	Green and white	1½ feet	Foliage	6
C	Dahlia	'Bonnie Esperance'	Dahlia	Soft pink	10 inches	Late summer– early fall	9
D	Butterfly Gladiolus		Gladiolus	Mixed: pinks, yellows, reds	2½–3 feet	Mid–late summer	16
E	Lily	'Connecticut Beauty'	Lilium	Soft yellow with orange and gold	3 feet	Late June–early July	10
F	Tuberose	'Excelsior Dwarf Pearl'	Polianthes tuberosa	White	2–3 feet	Late summer	12
G	Lily Turf	'Big Blue'	Liriope	Lavender-blue	12–15 inches	Late summer	10

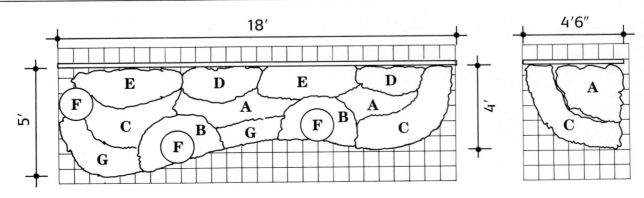

A FALL-BLOOMING BULB GARDEN

Tuck this pretty grouping in a place where you can enjoy it at close range. The large crocus flowers come in soft shades of rose, violet, and lilac. *Ceratostigma* provides an attractive background for the flowers, hides the ripening foliage, and provides a pretty show of bronze foliage and electric blue flowers in late summer and fall.

Colchicums and fall-flowering crocuses come as a delightful surprise in the autumn landscape. As seasonal accents, they liven up a border or any corner of the garden that needs a lift with fresh color. Massed or naturalized, these bulbs provide an unusual fall display.

Colchicums and fall-blooming crocuses are easy to grow. Like spring-flowering bulbs, they are dormant throughout the summer and are ready for planting in the fall. The difference is that the fall bulbs flower almost immediately after planting. If planting is delayed, the bulbs may not bloom the first year.

Many fall-flowering bulbs, like colchicums and several of the crocuses, have blooms that appear in the garden without the benefit of accompanying leaves. The leaves are produced in early spring and disappear completely by summer. Because the leaves can be messy (some are nearly 2 feet tall, surprisingly), I recommend planting these bulbs in a groundcover that will detract from the ripening foliage in late spring, and provide a background for the flowers in fall. Both groups of bulbs increase rapidly. In a short time, they will create a breathtaking display. The stonecrop, in bloom for many months, weaves the other garden elements together as they come and go.

A FALL-BLOOMING BULB GARDEN

	COMMON NAME	VARIETY	SCIENTIFIC NAME	COLOR	HEIGHT	BLOOM	NUMBER OF BULBS
A	Stonecrop	'Autumn Joy'	*Sedum*	Rich pink to coppery red	2 feet	Late summer–early fall	6
B	Fall Crocus		*Crocus speciosus*	Violet-blue	4–6 inches	Late summer–early fall	36
C	Colchicum	'Waterlily'	*Colchicum*	Rosy lilac	10–12 inches	Late summer–early fall	3
D	Colchicum	'The Giant'	*Colchicum*	Lilac-pink	10–12 inches	Late summer–early fall	3
E	Leadwort		*Ceratostigma plumbaginoides*	Electric blue	8–12 inches	Late summer–early fall	9

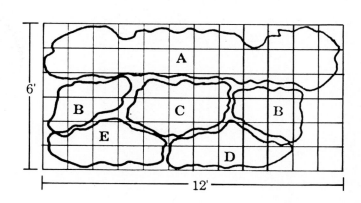

ROSE GARDENS

Beyond question, roses in their many forms are this country's favorite flower—in fact, the rose has recently been named the national flower. •The history of roses can be traced back to 2300 B.C., and these flowers are referred to in every period of man's recorded history: in ancient parchments from Asia and Europe, from Egyptian texts to Chinese holy writings. From ancient Greece to our day, troubadours and poets have lauded the rose and consequently it remains the symbol and messenger of love and tenderness. Nothing rivals the rose for beauty and fragrance, and no other flower contributes such a delightful sense of romance to a garden.

Hybrid teas are the flowers most of us think of when we hear the word "rose"—great big beauties, so treasured for cutting. Theoretically, hybrid teas are bushes with flowers borne singly on their stems.

Floribundas are charming and very versatile roses, producing large clusters of flowers all summer long. Of medium height and graceful, bushy habit, they have long been popular in Europe, where they are used extensively for mass plantings.

Grandifloras are the result of crossing hybrid teas and floribundas. They tend to be more vigorous than either parent, and produce large, hybrid, tealike blooms all summer. Some grandifloras flower in small clusters, others produce individual blooms.

Shrub roses are grown primarily not for their flowers, but rather for their permanent landscape value. Unlike the hybrid teas which are grafted onto hardy, wild rose root stock, grandifloras, and floribundas, shrub roses require little spraying or pruning, and are exceptionally hardy; they are grown on their own roots, so even if a cold winter kills them back to the ground, they will come back, and add masses of color to your June landscape. In addition to their months of floral beauty, they're attractive for their foliage, and some produce colorful berries—called hips—in late fall and winter.

Roses thrive in average, well-drained soil. They need 4 to 6 hours of direct sunlight daily. Plant bushes away from large shrubs so that air may circulate freely around them.

Space climbing roses 8 to 10 feet apart. Set hybrid teas, grandifloras, and floribundas 2 to 3½ feet apart in cold climates and 3½ to 4 feet apart in mild climates. Dig the hole 6 inches deeper than the existing root system, providing enough width to hold the roots without crowding. Mix the soil with 25 percent peat moss before filling in the hole. Be sure to set the bud union 1 inch below the soil surface. (The bud union—the place where the plant has been grafted—is marked by a line and slight swelling.)

Newly planted roses should not be fertilized until they are fully leafed out and growing steadily. Water well. Use a good commercial slow-release rose fertilizer (5–10–5), and do not let fertilizer touch stems or leaves. Fertilize three times a year: November (after plants enter their dormant stage); spring (when new growth is 4 inches long); and July (after the first significant blooming period).

Keep roses well fed and well watered, and remove faded and fallen leaves and petals regularly. Cover rose beds with a 2- to 3-inch layer of buckwheat hulls, shredded leaf mulch or fine wood chips. Well-rotted horse or cow manure provides a wonderful, rich mulch that roses love. However, it is very acid, and should be covered with a dusting of lime to balance it. Apply in early summer.

Throughout the growing season, treat bushes with a rose spray or dust formulated to control insects and disease. Apply early in the day once a week; during very hot weather apply every 2 weeks and after rain showers. In the fall, spray canes and surrounding areas with fungicide and insecticide.

Prune before buds begin to swell in spring; remove dead and broken canes. After growth begins, winter injuries can be identified and removed.

The red climbing rose 'Blaze' gives a romantic look to a trellis. Pink 'Simplicity' is the center of an herb garden.

ROSE GARDEN AT THE END OF A LAWN

This is a small rose garden featuring hybrid teas, floribundas, a grandiflora, and a shrub rose.

This garden features the hybrid tea 'Brandy' with long, slender, coppery orange buds that open to perfectly formed 4-inch flowers of tawny gold mellowing to apricot. Growing to 5 feet, it is a prolific bloomer, with glossy leaves and good disease resistance.

The other hybrid tea used in this garden is 'Peace'—the uncontested champion of the rose world since its introduction by the Meilland family in 1945. Large flowers open golden yellow flushed with pink, set against a background of lustrous, dark-green leaves. It is a 6-foot plant, extremely hardy, and a most generous bloomer.

'Sun Flare' is an outstanding floribunda producing masses of radiant lemon yellow, semi-double blooms in clusters of three to twelve. Glossy foliage on 2- to 3-foot plants plus a mild licorice fragrance make this rose an appealing addition to the garden. 'French Lace' also adds a pleasant, spicy fragrance. The blooms are ivory-colored, sometimes tinted with pink. As many as eight are borne on a single stem, and they appear repeatedly throughout the summer.

'Queen Elizabeth', the matriarch of all grandiflora roses, produces a profusion of classic, high-centered blooms, both singly and in clusters, well into the fall. The color is pink and the fragrance delicate. This regal beauty grows to a height of about 5 feet, and is increasing in popularity every year.

For this garden I chose the shrub rose 'Bonica' with its soft pink, fully double blooms coming in clusters of up to 20 flowers throughout the season. New side branches produce even more blooms, and bright red hips extend the show well into winter. It grows to 5 feet tall with an equal spread and is clad in deep, glossy green foliage.

The roses in this garden have been carefully selected and situated to produce a harmonious blend of pink, ivory, and yellow from late spring well into fall. The garden has been designed to be displayed against a dark green hedge of yew or holly but it will also be effective set against a wall or fence. Choose a location in full sun—at least 6 hours each day—where air circulates freely. Roses resent root competition, so try to keep your garden away from big trees.

Rose 'Queen Elizabeth'

Rose 'Brandy'

Rose 'Peace'

Rose 'Sun Flare'

Rose 'Bonica'

Rose 'French Lace'

	COMMON NAME	TYPE OF ROSE	VARIETY	SCIENTIFIC NAME	COLOR	HEIGHT	BLOOM	NUMBER OF PLANTS
	A ROSE GARDEN AT THE END OF A LAWN							
A	Rose	Floribunda	'Sun Flare'	*Rosa*	Lemon yellow	3–4 feet	June–frost	2
B	Rose	Shrub Rose	'Bonica'	*Rosa*	Soft pink	4–5 feet	June–frost	2
C	Rose	Floribunda	'French Lace'	*Rosa*	Ivory with pink or apricot	3–4 feet	June–frost	1
D	Rose	Hybrid Tea	'Peace'	*Rosa*	Golden yellow with pink	6 feet	June–frost	2
E	Rose	Grandiflora	'Queen Elizabeth'	*Rosa*	Tender pink	5–6 feet	June–frost	2
F	Rose	Hybrid Tea	'Brandy'	*Rosa*	Coppery orange to gold and apricot	5 feet	June–frost	1

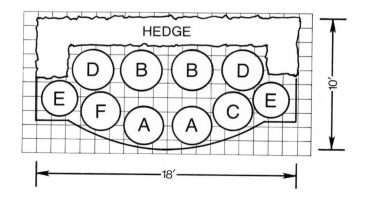

A FORMAL ROSE GARDEN

Roses lend themselves to a formal garden plan. This square garden is enclosed by a fence that supports climbing roses; the beds are laid out geometrically within. The arbor and bench are elements that add formality to the design.

These roses have been carefully selected and arranged to provide a harmonious blend of color from late spring to fall. They will need a location in full sun (at least 6 hours per day), away from tree roots, where air circulates freely. The candytuft, an evergreen perennial that flowers in June, is an edging that ties the beds together. Any type of open fencing, 3 to 4 feet high, may be used to enclose the garden.

A classic border of hybrid tea roses

A FORMAL ROSE GARDEN

	COMMON NAME	VARIETY	SCIENTIFIC NAME	COLOR	HEIGHT	BLOOM	NUMBER OF PLANTS
A	Hybrid Tea Rose	'Honor'	*Rosa*	White	3 feet	June–frost	3
B	Hybrid Tea Rose	'Oregold'	*Rosa*	Golden yellow	4 feet	June–frost	3
C	Hybrid Tea Rose	'Sheer Bliss'	*Rosa*	Creamy white with pink blush	1½–2 feet	June–frost	3
D	Hybrid Tea Rose	'Sweet Surrender'	*Rosa*	Silvery pink	3–4 feet	June–frost	3
E	Climbing Rose	'Climbing Peace'	*Rosa*	Golden yellow with pink	8–10 feet	June–frost	4
F	Climbing Rose	'Climbing Rhonda'	*Rosa*	Medium pink with coral overtones	8–10 feet	June–frost	2
G	Climbing Rose	'Golden Showers'	*Rosa*	Bright yellow	8–10 feet	June–frost	2
H	Climbing Rose	'America'	*Rosa*	Coral-pink	8–10 feet	June–frost	2
J	Candytuft	'Purity'	*Iberis sempervirens*	White	2 feet	June–frost	2

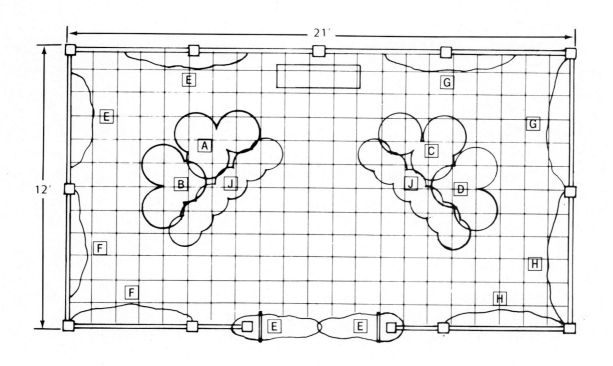

SHADE GARDENS

To many people, shade is very welcome, particularly on a hot, sunny day. Few plants will tolerate total shade, however. If you have lots of shade, be prepared to trim some branches to allow light and air to penetrate. Good drainage, too, is as essential in shade as it is in sun. But tree roots can create a difficult situation for plants. Add plenty of organic matter to the soil to help retain moisture. Prepare the garden as described in the introduction to annual flower gardens, page 11.

Once you have considered the special needs of the shady plants, your shady spot will be suitable for the plants shown in the following two designs.

White impatiens, variegated and green hostas, and blue pansies brighten up a shady spot.

A shady area becomes a rainbow of colors when planted with mixed astilbes.

A PARTIAL SHADE GARDEN

This shady alcove was designed for a small space in front of a large, old pine tree. The garden blooms from June through September, providing a colorful, refreshing place to sit on a hot summer day. It receives a half-day of direct sun: 4 to 6 hours. All but one of the seeds may be sown directly in the garden after the danger of frost is past; coleus should be started indoors. Nicotiana has very fine seed; in areas prone to heavy rains where seed might wash away, you may prefer to start them indoors.

To prepare for planting, we removed the lower branches of the pine tree, creating enough sun for flowers to bloom and flourish. We added three inches of topsoil throughout the garden; that way, we could plant without interfering with the roots of the pine tree. A seat was put at the back of the garden to provide a place to sit and enjoy the view.

The center of this garden could vary: it can be more formal and permanent with brick or flagstone, or informal with grass, pine needles, bark mulch, or wood chips. Pine needles have a wonderful fragrance, and you can probably find a place to rake and collect them at no expense. Both bark mulch and wood chips are available from your local garden center. The mulch will have to be replaced from time to time. I prefer a very finely chopped bark or wood chip mulch because it is in scale for a small garden.

A brick or wood edging is a very attractive feature and also helps keep the mulch in place. The bricks can be laid in a row, half-buried to keep them stable. The wood edging can be railroad ties or strips of two-by-fours anchored in the ground.

Many annuals grow well in shade. Feel free to be creative and substitute your favorites. The list of partial-shade-loving annuals includes begonias, impatiens, flowering maples, ageratums, salvias, and browallias, among others.

A Partial Shade Garden

A PARTIAL SHADE GARDEN

	COMMON NAME	VARIETY	SCIENTIFIC NAME	COLOR	HEIGHT	BLOOM	NUMBER OF SEED PACKETS
A	Cleome	'Queen'	*Cleome*	Mixed	4 feet	Summer to fall	1
B	Nasturtium	'Double Dwarf Jewel, Golden'	*Tropaeolum*	Yellow	1 feet	Summer	4
C	Bells of Ireland		*Molucella laevis*	Green	2½ feet	Summer	2
D	Flowering Tobacco	'Nicki Hybrid'	*Nicotiana*	White	2 feet	Summer to fall	1
E	Cosmos	'Sensation'	*Cosmos bipinnatus*	Mixed	4 feet	Summer to fall	1
F	Coleus	'Wizard Jade'	*Coleus*	Green, ivory	10 inches	Summer to fall	1

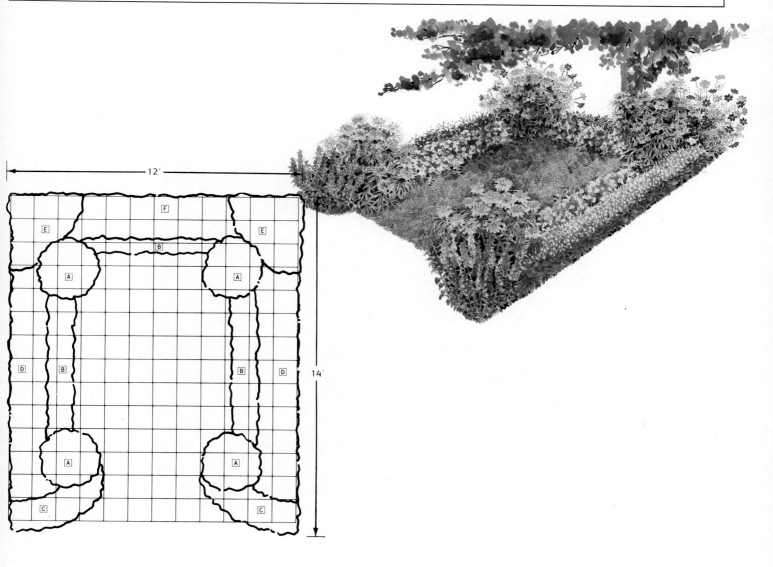

A WOODLAND SHADE GARDEN

Originally, I designed this shady garden for a couple who bought a wooded property, cleared an area for the house, and then wanted to have a garden in the woods that remained. We agreed that a path through the trees planted with shade-loving flowers was exactly what they needed. The garden combination of bulb and perennial will provide a wonderful contrast of foliage and color for three seasons.

The design is appropriate for an area with light, filtered light, and good topsoil. The light should be bright but not direct, although the plants will tolerate some early-morning or late-afternoon sun. Your best results will come if you provide these conditions.

Select a location, ideally a spot in the dappled shade of light-canopied deciduous trees. The design is very informal and flexible: you can simply wind a curved path, 3 to 5 feet wide, between the existing trees and shrubs. Lay out the sections of the design far enough from the trees and shrubs to avoid their roots, and try to stay away from trees with massive root systems near the surface. Heavy feeders like beech and maple should be avoided.

The planting plan reflects the mature size of the plants, allowing room for growth. The garden will take a year or two to fill out, depending on what size perennials you plant. The perennials will grow and spread, so that in a few years you will be able to dig and divide them.

The bulbs of tuberous begonias and caladiums are not hardy, and must be lifted in the fall after the first frost and stored in a dark, dry place until the following spring. Then they can be potted up for an early start indoors, or they can be planted directly in the garden once spring frost is past.

A WOODLAND SHADE GARDEN

	COMMON NAME	VARIETY	SCIENTIFIC NAME	COLOR	HEIGHT	BLOOM	NUMBER OF BULBS OR PLANTS
A	Hardy Amaryllis		*Lycoris squamigera*	Lavender with pink	2–3 feet	Late summer	12
B	Windflower	'St. Brigid'	*Anemone blanda*	Mixed	1 foot	Spring	50
C	Astilbe	'Bonn'	*Astilbe*	Pink	24–30 inches	June	6
D	Tuberous Begonia	'Nonstop Hybrid'	*Begonia*	Mixed	8–12 inches	June–frost	60
E	Bleeding Heart		*Dicentra spectabilis*	Pink	4 feet	Spring	12
F	Caladium	'Candidum'	*Caladium*	White with green	1½ feet	Foliage	12
G	Columbine	'McKana's Giant'	*Aquilegia*	Mixed	2½ feet	Spring	15
H	Daylily	'Hyperion'	*Hemerocallis*	Yellow	3½ feet	Summer	10
J	Shield Fern		*Dryopteris marginalis*	Green	1½–2 feet	Foliage	15
K	Hosta	'Royal Standard'	*Hosta*	Green foliage, lavender flower	2-foot flower	Summer	25
L	Lily Turf	'Majestic'	*Liriope*	Green foliage, violet flower	10 inches	Late summer	12
M	Lily of the Valley		*Convallaria majalis*	White	9 inches	Spring	150
N	Primrose	'Dwarf Jewel'	*Primula*	Mixed	6 inches	Spring	21
O	Violet	'Helen Mount'	*Viola*	Tricolor	10 inches	Spring–fall	15

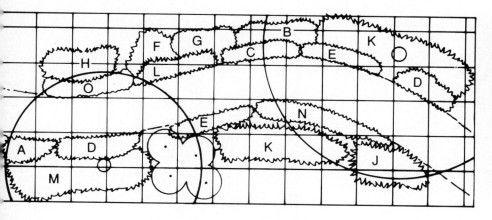

This shady woodland path is lined with liriope, and filled with columbines, geraniums, and bleeding hearts, among others.

COMBINATION GARDENS

These gardens have a mixture of seasonal bloom. Many of them provide three seasons of color, from spring through fall. Most include a combination of seeds, bulbs, and plants.

The plans can be used in various spots on your property. You might try "A Tranquil Spot" against a garage wall or your neighbor's fence. The "White Fragrance Garden" would be lovely between two large shrubs or near a gazebo. The "Salad Garden" is a natural choice to plant by your kitchen door, and the "Herb Garden" would add charm and interest to a secluded, sunny spot. Prepare your garden for planting as described in the introduction to annual flower gardens, page 11.

Annuals and perennials blooming together provide a long season of color. Featured here, from bottom: ageratums, dusty miller, coreopsis, German irises, daylilies, cosmos, and Queen Anne's lace.

A TRANQUIL SPOT

So many times the garage wall in a backyard is not very attractive. Here is a plan for that wall. With the addition of a bench and two beds of flowers on each side, you can make this a most attractive spot.

The varieties of tulips and perennials in this garden have been selected to provide a succession of bloom from spring into fall, as well as foliage that has attractive color and texture throughout the growing season. Choose a location that receives at least 6 hours of full sun each day.

In the spring, the bulbs begin with the tulip Kaufmanniana which is 6 to 8 inches tall, a soft yellow touched with rosy red outside, creamy white with gold inside shaped like a water lily.

Next comes tulip 'Hocus Pocus' with its large, deep cups of gleaming yellow; the inner petals have a crimson streak partly concealed by the outer petals. It is magnificent in form and glorious in color.

'Sweet Harmony', a single late tulip, has a very soft blending of pale lemon yellow and creamy white.

Bergenia cordifolia is an evergreen perennial with leathery leaves that are about 18 inches tall. Its pink flowers bloom in June.

In spring, after the bulbs have finished blooming, clip off the dead flowers to prevent seed formation, but do not remove the leaves until they have turned yellow. This is the time to interplant annuals among the tulips to provide additional summer color with the perennials.

In summer, 'Munstead' lavender provides silvery foliage and lavender flowers. This aromatic, shrubby perennial is valuable as a low hedge, in the herb garden, or the front border. The dried flowers are prized for sachets and potpourris.

The aster 'Wonder of Staffa' is on practically every expert's list of ten best perennials. Blooming from July to November, 2-foot plants dependably produce spikes of lavender-blue flowers.

Purple loosestrife is a showy, easy-to-grow plant. 'Morden's Pink' has a dense, bushy habit, growing 3 to 4 feet tall and bearing spikes of deep pink flowers from June to September. It thrives in rich, moist soil. Loosestrife is extremely hardy, heat- and drought-resistant. Naturalized along the roadside, loosestrife is very invasive; 'Morden's Pink', which is sterile, is a good garden variety, not badly behaved as other loosestrifes are.

The sedum, 'Autumn Joy', is widely acclaimed as one of the best perennials and has year 'round value in the border. It quickly forms a handsome, 2-foot-tall clump of toothed, silver-green, fleshy leaves, beautiful throughout the summer. In late summer, large, flat heads of deep pink flowers appear, turning to salmon-bronze and then coppery red as autumn progresses.

The returning perennials make this a very easy garden to maintain, and the bulbs and annuals can provide an interesting change.

Tulip kaufmanniana

Tulip 'Hocus Pocus'

Tulip 'Sweet Harmony'

Bergenia

Lavender 'Munstead'

Aster 'Wonder of Staffa'

Stonecrop 'Autumn Joy'

Loosestrife 'Rose Queen'

A TRANQUIL SPOT

	COMMON NAME	VARIETY	SCIENTIFIC NAME	COLOR	HEIGHT	BLOOM	NUMBER OF BULBS OR PLANTS
A	Tulip	'Kaufmanniana'	*Tulipa kaufmanniana*	Creamy white, soft yellow, and rosy red	6 inches	March–early April	24
B	Tulip	'Hocus Pocus'	*Tulipa Single Late*	Gleaming yellow, with crimson streaks	28–30 inches	May	12
C	Tulip	'Sweet Harmony'	*Tulipa Single Late*	Pale lemon yellow and white	2 feet	May	12
D	Bergenia		*Bergenia cordifolia*	Lavender-pink with green	1½ feet	Mid-spring	10
E	Lavender	'Munstead'	*Lavendula augustifolia*	Lavender	1 foot	June–July	2
F	Aster	'Wonder of Staffa'	*Aster x. frikartii*	Lavender blue	1½–2 feet	July–November	6
G	Loosestrife	'Morden's Pink'	*Lythrum salicaria*	Dark pink	1½ feet	June–September	4
H	Stonecrop	'Autumn Joy'	*Sedum purpureum*	Pink to red	2 feet	Late summer–early fall	6

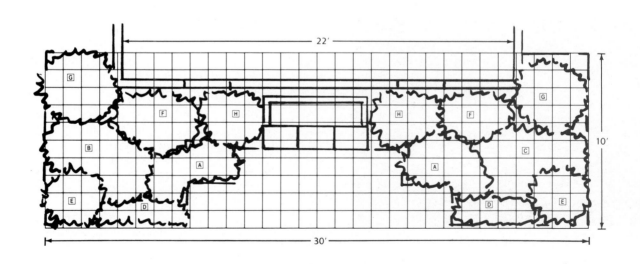

A WHITE FRAGRANCE GARDEN

This garden is designed to please the eye and scent the air. Plant it between two fragrant, blooming shrubs such as mock orange (*Philadelphus*) and butterfly bush (*Buddleia*) for maximum fragrance. This garden will bloom in sequence for about 3 months, from mid-spring to mid-summer. It starts with daffodils and hyacinths, and ends with August-blooming lilies. You could add masses of flowering tobacco (*Nicotiana*) once the spring bulbs fade.

A WHITE FRAGRANCE GARDEN

	COMMON NAME	VARIETY	SCIENTIFIC NAME	COLOR	HEIGHT	BLOOM	NUMBER OF PLANTS
A	Daffodil	'Mount Hood'	*Narcissus*	White and pale yellow	1½ feet	April	48
B	Daffodil	'Geranium'	*Narcissus*	White with orange	1–1½ feet	Late season	24
C	Daffodil	'Thalia'	*Narcissus*	White	12–15 inches	Late mid-season	24
D	Hyacinth	'L'innocence'	*Hyacinthus orientalis*	Pure white	10 inches	April	12
E	Candytuft	'Purity'	*Iberis sempervirens*	White	10 inches	Mid-spring	9
F	Lily	'Madonna'	*Lilium*	Waxy white with yellow anthers	2–4 feet	June–early July	18
G	Hardy Amaryllis		*Lycoris squamigera*	Lavender-pink	2–3 feet	Late summer	6
H	Regal Lily	'Regale'	*Lilium regale*	White, lilac-pink	4 feet	July–August	18

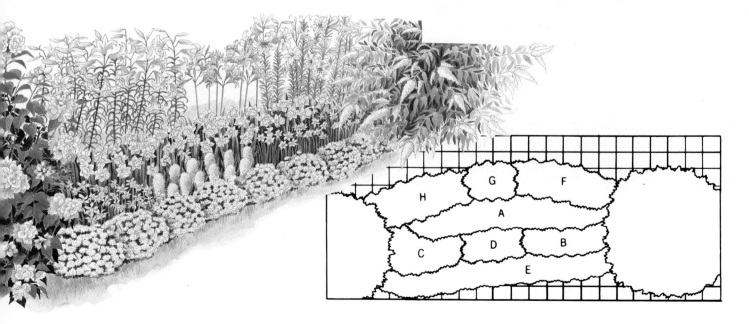

A SALAD GARDEN BY THE KITCHEN DOOR

This attractive garden will provide an abundance of greens, radishes, and tomatoes for tasty salads. Plant it near the kitchen door, or in any other convenient location that receives at least 4 hours of direct sun each day. All of these seeds may be direct sown in the prepared garden. Lettuce and radishes grow best in cold weather and should be sown as soon as the soil can be worked; plant tomatoes, dill, and nasturtiums when the soil is warm and after all danger of frost has passed. Basket tomato 'King Hybrid' was developed especially for outdoor sowing, and will bear fruit very early.

You may find the following Burpee products helpful in growing your salad garden:

The Lawn and Garden Blanket® is used by commercial growers for seed protection and to encourage early germination and fast plant growth. It also protects plants from insect damage. Blankets are now available for home gardeners. They are reusable.

Tomato cages can be placed around each young tomato plant; the cages keep fruit off the ground and improve exposure to the sun. These galvanized wire cages fold flat for storage.

Foam plant ties are flexible, plastic foam-covered wire that is soft and won't damage plants. They are durable and reusable.

*A Salad Garden by
the Kitchen Door*

A SALAD GARDEN BY THE KITCHEN DOOR

	COMMON NAME	VARIETY	NUMBER OF SEEDLINGS
A	Parsley	'Extra Curled Dwarf'	14
B	Radish	'Cherry Belle'	Seed
C	Garden Cress		Seed
D	Lettuce	'Loosehead Blend'	1 dozen
E	Lettuce	'Great Lakes'	1 dozen
F	Lettuce	'Green Ice'	1 dozen
G	Nasturtium	'Double Dwarf Jewel Mixed'	2 dozen
H	Dill		5
I	Tomato	'Basket King Hybrid'	3

When planting from seed: use 1 seed packet for each variety.

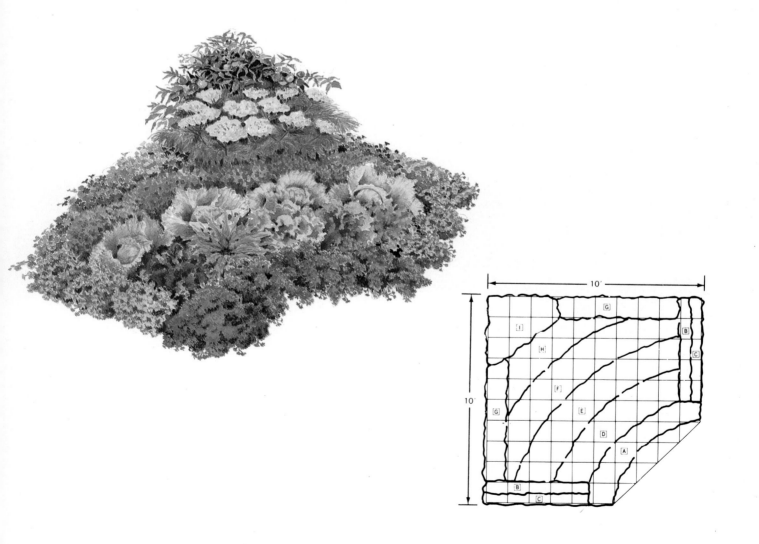

AN HERB GARDEN

This herb garden is easy to grow and combines attractive color and texture with appealing fragrance. It will produce an abundance of herbs to use fresh throughout the summer and fall, or to dry for winter. It can be situated near a building or fence—any location that receives at least 6 hours of sun each day.

The herbs in this garden add delicious flavor and aroma to even the most everyday dishes. When seasoning foods, try substituting herbs for salt. Pick the herbs as needed for fresh use—preferably in the morning, just after the dew has dried on the leaves, for the fullest flavor. To harvest herbs for drying, cut them when the leaves have the highest oil content—usually just before flowering (chamomile and summer savory are exceptions, and should be cut in full flower). Herbs are easily dried; tie them in bunches and hang in a shaded, well-ventilated place. When thoroughly dry, store the leaves in glass jars or tightly sealed plastic bags in a dry, dark place. All of these herbs can be picked all summer long, often into fall, depending on where you live.

	COMMON NAME	SCIENTIFIC NAME	COLOR	HEIGHT	NUMBER OF PLANTS
			AN HERB GARDEN		
A	Lavender	*Lavendula angustifolia*	Purple	2½ feet	3
B	Spearmint	*Mentha spicata*	Purple	2–3 feet	3
C	Sweet Marjoram	*Origanum majarana*	White or pink	2 feet	3
D	Dill	*Anethum graveolens*	Yellow	3 feet	3
E	Rosemary	*Rosmarinus officinalis*	Silver foliage	2–3 feet	3
F	Thyme	*Thymus vulgaris*	Pale purple	6–12 inches	3
G	Sweet Basil	*Ocinum basilicum*	White	1–1½ feet	3
H	Sage	*Salvia officinalis*	Silver-green foliage	1–2 feet	3
J	Chives	*Allium schoenoprasum*	Lavender-purple flowers with green foliage	1–1½ feet	3
K	Curled Parsley	*Petroselinum crispum*	Green foliage	10 inches	3

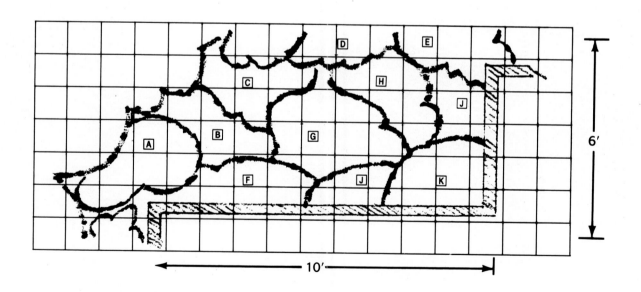

PERENNIAL GARDENS

Unlike annuals, perennials are plants that continue to grow in the garden year after year. They increase in size, so be sure to allow plenty of room around each plant. It is wise to keep a plan of the garden so you can check your plants every spring as growth starts. If any plants have not survived (because of severe weather or damage by mice, for example), you will be able to determine which they are by consulting the plan. And, after several years, some perennials will have to be divided.

Careful soil preparation is essential for a perennial garden because it assures years of good growth and beauty. Soil composition cannot be successfully altered once long-lived perennials have been planted. Soil should be prepared a week or more before planting. For best results, test the pH factor. You can send soil samples to your local county extension agent, or purchase an inexpensive home soil-testing kit or battery-operated pH meter. Most perennials prefer a neutral pH. If the soil is too acid, add ground limestone at the rate of 5 to 10 pounds per 100 square feet. If you have a heavy clay soil, add compost.

Spade the soil to a depth of at least 18 inches. Work in liberal amounts of organic matter like peat moss, leaf mold, compost, or well-rotted manure, plus a slow-release fertilizer. A good general fertilizer for perennials is 5–10–5, applied at the rate of about 4 pounds per 100 square feet or according to package directions.

Plant from late summer to early fall, or in late spring after the danger of frost is past. Spring planting is safer in areas where winters are severe. Set plants into the ground as soon as possible after arrival. If planting must be delayed a few days, place the plants in a cool, shaded area and keep the roots moist.

Dig holes large enough for the roots to spread out. Set plants with the crowns at or just below the soil level. Firm the soil around the roots by tramping on it or pressing very hard with your hands. Water well. These last two steps are essential to eliminate any air pockets around the roots.

Allow 2 to 3 feet between different types of plants for medium to tall varieties, 12 inches for smaller ones. Consult plant labels for the height of your plant at maturity.

Cultivate the perennial border in spring after the plants are well up, and once again 4 to 6 weeks later as they begin to bloom. Work the soil to a depth of 2 to 3 inches with a cultivator to destroy weeds and aerate the soil. Use fertilizer according to package directions.

Water plants deeply during dry spells, without letting them wilt. Water early in the day so leaves will dry off quickly. Wet foliage makes plants susceptible to fungus diseases.

After the second cultivating and fertilizing, mulch the soil between plants to keep down weeds and conserve moisture. Apply at least 2 inches of peat moss, grass clippings, compost, or any other material that will decompose over the course of the season.

In areas where there is danger of alternate freezing and thawing during the winter, mulch the ground around the plants in fall. After the soil has frozen, apply a layer of salt hay, straw, evergreen branches, or any other coarse, lightweight material to keep the soil at a constant or uniform temperature. This prevents heaving and thawing.

Annuals can be tucked into a perennial border for a lush look.

A PINK AND YELLOW SUMMER GARDEN

This summer garden is designed with hardy, long-blooming perennials. The plan combines pink and yellow flowers accented with clumps of variegated grass and mounds of artemisia for foliage and textural interest. You will enjoy an abundance of bloom from early summer well into fall with plenty for bouquets. This garden is suitable for many places in the landscape; as an island in a sunny yard, curved along a walk, or set at the back of a lawn. Straighten the lines if you prefer, and plant the garden along a south-facing wall or fence. Choose a location that receives full sun at least 6 hours each day.

Stonecrop 'Ruby Glow'

Bee balm 'Croftway Pink'

Pinks 'Helen'

Loosestrife 'Ruby Glow'

Maiden grass 'Morning Light'

Artemisia 'Silver Mound'

Coreopsis 'Moonbeam'

A PINK AND YELLOW SUMMER GARDEN

	Common Name	Variety	Scientific Name	Color	Height	Bloom	Number of Plants
A	Bee Balm	'Croftway Pink'	*Monarda didyma*	Salmon-rose	3–4 feet	June–September	6
B	Maiden Grass	'Morning Light'	*Miscanthus sinesis*	Silvery green and white	4–5 feet	Grown for foliage	4
C	Artemisia	'Silver Mound'	*Artemisia schmidtiana*	Silver	8–10 inches	Grown for foliage	10
D	Loosestrife	'Morden's Pink'	*Lythrum salicaria*	Rich pink	3–4 feet	June–September	3
E	Stonecrop	'Autumn Joy'	*Sedum purpureum*	Pink to red	2 feet	August–September	2
F	Coreopsis	'Moonbeam'	*Coreopsis verticillata*	Creamy yellow	1½–2 feet	June–September	5
G	Pinks	'Helen'	*Dianthus*	Salmon-pink	10–12 inches	June–September	8

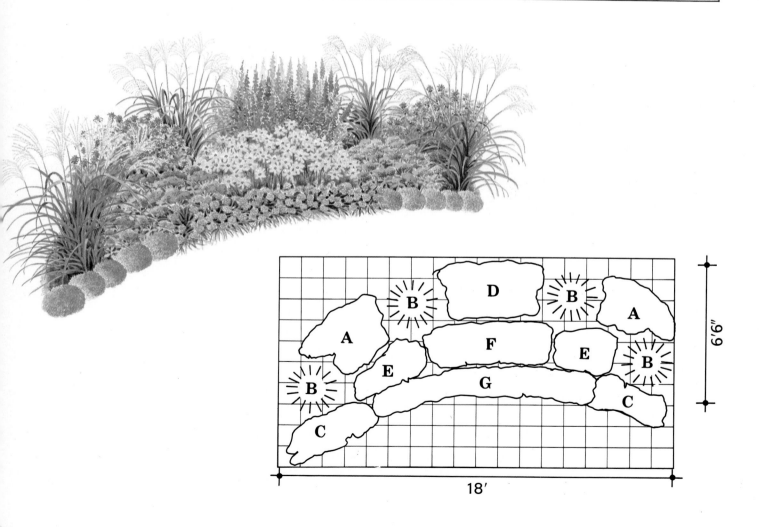

A DAISY GARDEN

The old song "Daisy, Daisy Give Me Your Answer True" was in my mind when I worked up this little garden with nine different daisy-type flowers.

Many of the daisy-flowered plants belong to the chrysanthemum family, but not all. Daisies are one of my favorite flowers, so I selected a group that includes plants from a number of different families. They are generally easy to grow, and are excellent as cut flowers. Some of them will bloom early (usually the shorter ones). Others flower well into fall, providing height and color at the back of the garden. The flowers vary in size from 1 to 4 inches. A range of colors is available, but I decided to stick primarily with yellows and whites in this garden.

Aurinia This low-growing plant is not a daisy, but I included it because it provides a nice early-flowering edging to the taller flowers and effectively pulls the different parts of the garden together.

Anthemis, 'Kelwayi' This hardy marguerite blooms all summer. It is very showy, with bright yellow 2-inch daisies, and is an excellent choice for cutting.

Aster x. frikartii This plant is rated one of the top ten perennials for its long bloom and easy care. From July to November, this 24-inch plant provides lavish 2½-inch lavender-blue flowers.

Border Mum, 'Golden Regards' This compact chrysanthemum, 8 to 10 inches tall, works well in the front of a border. It blooms well into the fall, carrying this garden through to the very

Gaillardia This plant produces bright daisy flowers profusely from June to frost. The blooms are colorful, in shades of red and yellow. Another good flower for cutting.

Heliopsis, 'Summer Sun' These small sunflowers are long-lasting and easy to grow, with 2-inch, soft-yellow flowers on 30-inch stems from August to October.

Peony, 'Edulis Superba' is a rosy pink, crowned with a tuft of short, shell pink flowers.

Rudbeckia hirta, 'Goldsturm Strain' This is the familiar black-eyed Susan; it is easy to grow and produces an abundance of long-lasting flowers. They are beautiful as cut flowers.

Rudbeckia hirta, 'Double Gold' 'Double Gold' is simply a double strain of the old-fashioned black-eyed Susan, with fuller flowers that look a bit like yellow zinnias. I included this plant because so many people love double flowers.

With these many varieties, there will always be one in bloom to pick and follow the old-fashioned saying, "she loves me, she loves me not" as you pluck each petal.

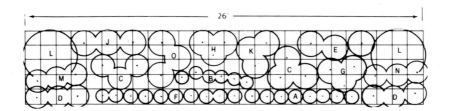

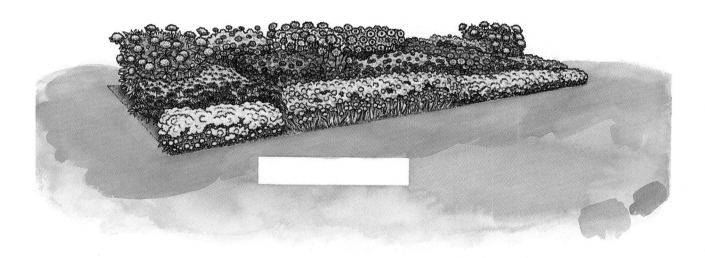

	COMMON NAME	VARIETY	SCIENTIFIC NAME	COLOR	HEIGHT	BLOOM	NUMBER OF PLANTS
				A DAISY GARDEN			
A	Basket of Gold	'Gold Dust'	*Aurinia saxatilis*	Golden yellow	1 foot	Early spring	9
B	Yellow Marguerite Daisy	'Kelwayi Yellow'	*Anthemis tinctoria*	Pure golden yellow	2 feet	June–frost	6
C	Aster	'Wonder of Staffa'	*Aster x. frikartii*	Lavender-blue	1½–2 feet	July–November	6
D	Border Mum	'Golden Regards'	*Chrysanthemum*	Golden yellow	8–10 inches	Fall	6
E	Coreopsis	'Sunray'	*Coreopsis grandiflora*	Golden yellow	1½ feet	June–September	3
F	Pinks	'Helen'	*Dianthus*	Salmon-pink	10–12 inches	June–September	9
G	Blanket Flower	'Goblin'	*Gaillardia grandiflora*	Red and yellow	1 foot	June–frost	3
H	Black-eyed Susan	'Double Gold'	*Rudbeckia hirta*	Golden yellow	3 feet	June–frost	3
J	False Sunflower	'Summer Sun'	*Heliopsis helianthoides*	Soft yellow	2½-feet	June–August	3
K	Painted Daisy		*Chrysanthemum coccineum*	Pink, rose, red, white	1½–2 feet	May–June	3
L	Peony	'Edulis Superba'	*Paeonia*	Rosy pink, shell pink	2½–3 feet	June	2
M	Black-eyed Susan	'Goldsturm'	*Rudbeckia hirta*	Deep yellow	2 feet	June–September	3
N	Shasta Daisy	'Starburst Hybrid'	*Chrysanthemum maximum*	White, yellow	1 foot	June–September	3
O	Shasta Daisy	'Silver Princess'	*Chrysanthemum maximum*	White	3½ feet	June–July	3

AN EARLY-BLOOMING PERENNIAL GARDEN FROM SEED

If you've never experienced the satisfaction of growing perennials from seed, here's a perennial border to try that will reward you with bloom the very first year. From late spring to late summer, it will provide an array of white, blue, yellow, and red flowers. For best results, start the seeds indoors 6 to 10 weeks before the last frost; if direct sown outdoors, you will enjoy fewer flowers the first year, but profuse blooms each year thereafter. The garden requires at least 6 hours of full sun each day and well-drained soil. This is a selection of long-lived, easy-to-grow perennials that you will enjoy year after year outdoors, as splendid plants, and indoors, as cut flowers.

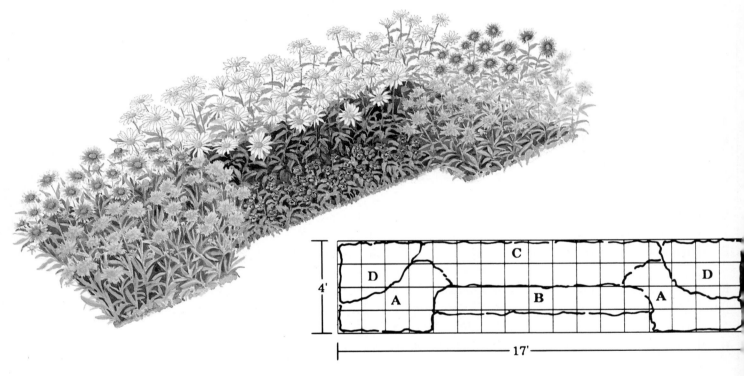

	COMMON NAME	VARIETY	SCIENTIFIC NAME	COLOR	HEIGHT	BLOOM
A	Coreopsis	'Early Sunrise'	*Coreopsis grandiflora*	Golden yellow	2 feet	June–September
B	Violet	'Princess Blue'	*Viola cornuta*	Violet-blue	6 inches	May–July
C	Shasta Daisy	'Starburst Hybrid'	*Chrysanthemum maximum*	White, yellow	1–1½ feet	June–September
D	Blanket Flower	'Portola Giants'	*Gaillardia grandiflora*	Bronzy scarlet with yellow	2½ feet	June–September

AN EARLY-BLOOMING PERENNIAL GARDEN FROM SEED

Use 1 seed packet for each variety.

A GARDEN OF PERENNIAL EVERLASTINGS

This plan, planted with perennial everlastings, differs from the garden of annual everlastings: The plants will come back next year and, in fact, they should continue to grow for many years.

The combination was designed for a sunny corner. The corners are planted with statice and salvia. In between, one of the grasses—low-growing blue fescue—makes a nice edging, with yarrow, sedum, and baby's breath behind.

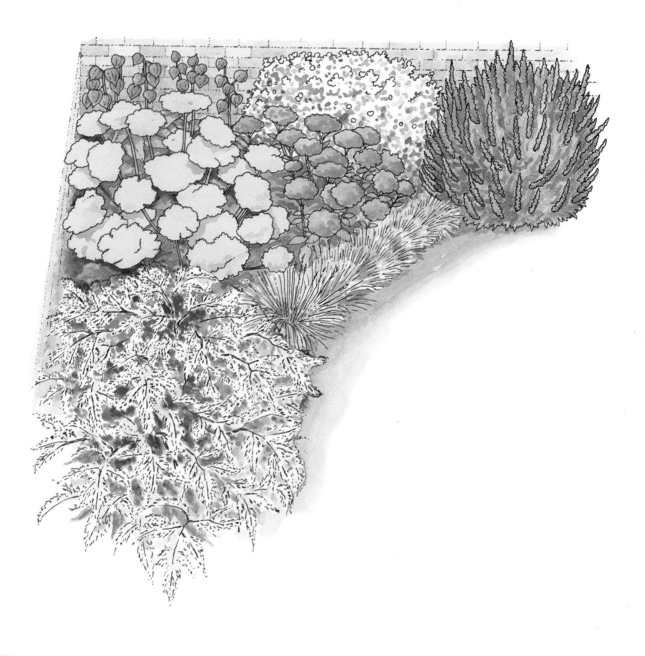

A GARDEN OF PERENNIAL EVERLASTINGS

	Common Name	Variety	Scientific Name	Color	Height	Bloom	Number of Seedling Plants
A	Statice		Limonium latifolia	Lavender, purple	2 feet	July–August	3
B	Yarrow	'Gold Plate'	Achillea filipendulina	Bright gold	3 feet	June–October	3
C	Stonecrop	'Autumn Joy'	Sedum purpureum	Pink to red	2 feet	August–September	3
D	Blue Fescue	'Azurit'	Feustuca cinerea	Silvery blue	10 inches	Grown for foliage	6
E	Chinese Lanterns		Physalis alkekengi	Orange-red	2 feet	September (pods ripen)	3
F	Baby's Breath	'Early Snowball'	Gypsophila elegans	White	3 feet	June–September	3
G	Meadow Sage	'Superba'	Salvia nemerosa	Violet-blue	2–3 feet	June–September	3

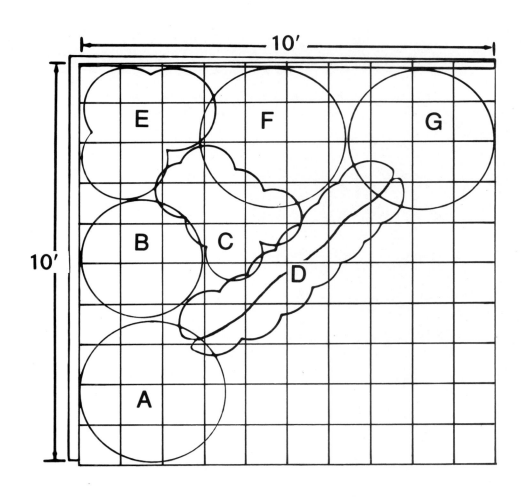

AN AUTUMN GARDEN FOR A TOWNHOUSE

Many townhouses, whether they be in large cities or country villages, have small areas by the steps which, with plantings, can be very attractive year 'round. With as few as 3 varieties of perennial, you can plan an effective end-of-the-season display. For this particular spot on a lovely city street, we concentrated on making a pretty garden to return to at the end of the summer.

The *Aster × frikartii* will be lovely for many weeks. The three varieties of chrysanthemums I have selected are about 1½ feet tall and have lovely colors. You might prefer to vary the plan with the many other varieties that are available.

The sedum, 'Autumn Joy', will grow 2 feet tall and bloom for many weeks, followed by coppery red seed pods that will keep their bronzy color all winter.

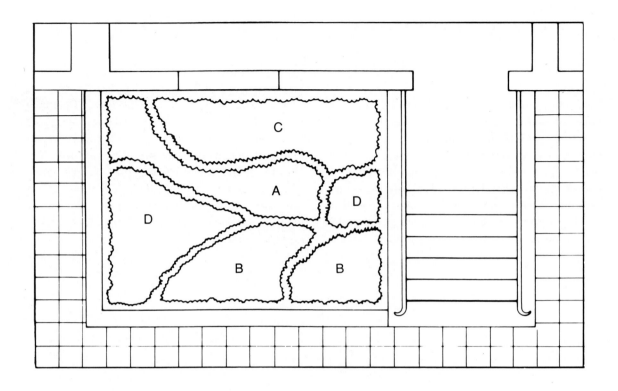

			AN AUTUMN GARDEN FOR A TOWNHOUSE				
	COMMON NAME	VARIETY	SCIENTIFIC NAME	COLOR	HEIGHT	BLOOM	NUMBER OF SEEDLING PLANTS
A	Aster	'Wonder of Staffa'	*Aster × frikartii*	Lavender-blue	1½–2 feet	July–November	7
B	Cushion Mum	'Powder River'	*Chrysanthemum*	Pure white	1 foot	August–September	6
C	Garden Mum	'New Firebird'	*Chrysanthemum*	Crimson	2½–3 feet	September–October	6
D	Stonecrop	'Autumn Joy'	*Sedum purpureum*	Rich pink to coppery-red	2 feet	August–September	11

ORNAMENTAL GRASSES

I designed this garden in front of a lovely water view, because I believe that grasses are particularly suited to such a situation. This collection, which includes both ornamental grasses and artemisia, would also make a handsome planting in front of a low wall or fence. From late spring through fall, you can enjoy the pleasing contrast of soft chartreuse *Sesleria* against silver-blue *Helictotrichon* and the silvery mounds of artemisia. Even in winter, grasses provide interest; the seeds last for a long time, and the stems catch and sculpt the snow. Choose a location that receives full sun, at least 6 hours each day.

Ornamental Grasses

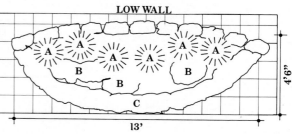

ORNAMENTAL GRASSES					
COMMON NAME	VARIETY	SCIENTIFIC NAME	COLOR	HEIGHT	NUMBER OF PLANTS
A Blue Oat Grass		*Helictotrichon sempervirens*	Silver blue	2 feet	6
B Autumn Moor Grass		*Sesleria autumnalis*	Chartreuse	1 foot	4
C Artemisia	'Silver Mound'	*Artemisia schmidtiana*	Silver	8–10 inches	10

CONTAINER GARDENS

Many different kinds of containers are available for planting, from rough, wooden boxes or barrels to beautiful lead pots. For a particularly important spot, I suggest purchasing a container that will look well throughout the year. If you're planning an informal, planting—of herbs, for example—a simple, inexpensive container like a whiskey barrel will do. Terra cotta chimney tiles also make attractive, inexpensive containers. (They are available at masonry supply yards and can be bought in a great variety of lengths.) I have one 18 inches high by 18 inches square in a dark corner of my yard where the fence joins the house, and it has lasted for many years. It holds a climbing hydrangea, which has spread to both the house wall and the fence. The plant doesn't need extra watering, just feeding in the early spring.

Terrace containers should be mobile, so it is wise to keep them on platforms with wheels. Make sure that the container has several drainage holes in the bottom. Cover the holes with pieces of broken clay pot and fill with a soilless or sterilized, porous potting mixture. Place the container in full spring sun.

Fall planting. Lay the bulbs on the soil according to your planting plan. Space them evenly in their allotted sections so that they are almost touching, then cover each bulb with the appropriate amount of soil.

Winter care. Soil in containers freezes more easily than soil in the ground. Container-grown plants need extra winter protection, therefore. South of Zone 7, bulbs in containers usually winter-over satisfactorily without extra protection. North of Zone 7, they should be protected. Straw, leaves, or even newspaper can be mounded over and around the container and then anchored with a tarp or heavy piece of plastic. Make some holes in the cover to allow for air circulation. Alternatively, if moving is practical, the container can be placed in a cool shed, garage, or enclosed porch. Ideally, the place should be below 40 degrees Fahrenheit, but rarely subjected to severe freezing. Be sure to keep the soil moist.

Spring care. After danger of severe freezing is past and growth begins to show in spring, remove the layer of protective covering. If your bulbs wintered-over on a porch, move the container out to a sunny location. Feed with a special fertilizer like Holland Bulb Booster™. If rainfall is insufficient, water deeply, and continue to do so throughout the period of active growth and bloom. Do not cut the foliage until it turns yellow. After that, the bulbs may be lifted and stored in paper or net bags in a well-ventilated place at about 70 degrees Fahrenheit until September.

Follow-up summer bloom. If you do not want to lift your bulbs, by all means overplant them with petunias, geraniums, or other annuals for continued color throughout the summer.

Combinations. The combinations shown here are just some of many you could use. If you are going to replace the bulbs with annuals, select something like the green and white vinca that will trail and soften the edges of the container. Fill the containers with colorful plants that vary in height to make it look like a real garden in miniature.

Pots overflowing with annuals are an easy way to decorate a deck.

DAFFODIL FESTIVAL

This garden in miniature, designed for a round container approximately 4 feet in diameter and at least 12 inches deep, will provide a splash of color and fragrance for about four weeks begin-ning in mid-spring. The daffodils will open in sequence, with some overlapping of bloom time, while the *scilla* creates a pretty contrasting bor-der of blue.

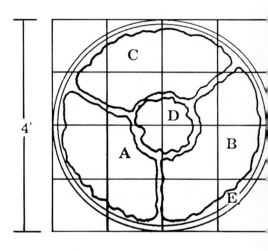

			DAFFODIL FESTIVAL				
	COMMON NAME	VARIETY	SCIENTIFIC NAME	COLOR	HEIGHT	BLOOM	NUMBER OF BULBS
A	Daffodil	'Pipit'	*Narcissus*	Lemon yellow to ivory	1–1½ feet	Mid-season	6
B	Daffodil	'Ice Wings'	*Narcissus*	White	6–8 inches	Late season	6
C	Daffodil	'Geranium'	*Narcissus*	White with orange	14 inches	Late season	6
D	Daffodil	'Tahiti'	*Narcissus*	Bright yellow to deep orange	1½ feet	Mid-season	6
E	Siberian Squill	'Spring Beauty'	*Scilla siberica*	Blue	4–6 inches	Mid-season	48

TULIP MEDLEY

This enchanting tulip display, designed for a rectangular container approximately 6 feet long by 2 feet wide and at least 12 inches deep, will bloom for 6 weeks beginning in early spring. 'Heart's Delight' opens first, followed by 'Angelique', and finally the *Scilla campanulata*. Plant the bulbs in late September (or as soon afterwards as possible), to allow ample time for good root development before frost. Container-grown bulbs need at least a month of moderately cool (but above freezing) temperatures to establish strong root systems.

Tulip 'Heart's Delight'

Wood hyacinth 'Blue Excelsior'

Tulip 'Angelique'

TULIP MEDLEY

	Common Name	Variety	Scientific Name	Color	Height	Bloom	Number of Bulbs
A	Tulip	'Angelique'	*Tulipa*	Pink	1½ feet	Late spring	12
B	Wood Hyacinth	'Blue Excelsior'	*Scilla campanulata*	Lilac with blue	1½ feet	Late May	12
C	Tulip	'Heart's Delight'	*Tulipa kaufmanniana*	Pink, red with yellow	10–12 inches	Late March–early April	12

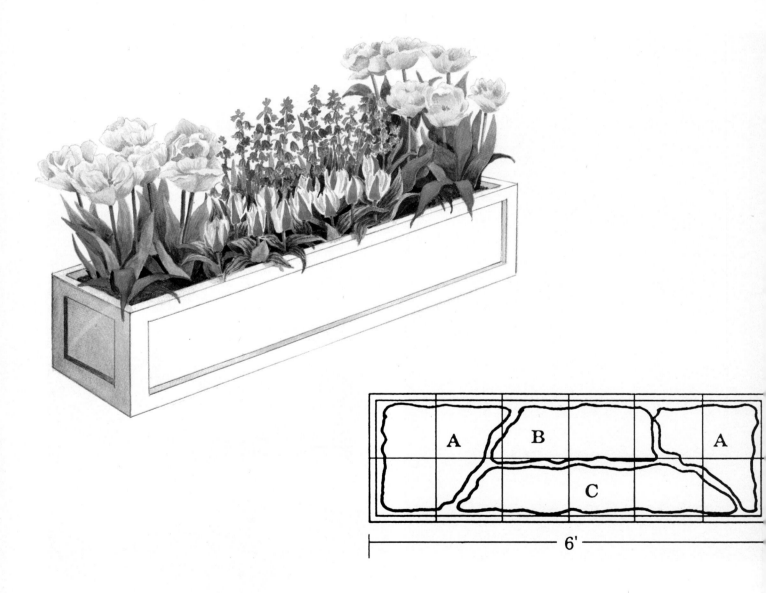

SPRING HARMONY

This rectangular container with its three varieties of bulbs begins with early *Leucojum*, 'Summer Snowflake', a lovely sight in late May, with clusters of bells on 18-inch stems.

The *Allium moly*, which blooms at about the same time, has yellow flowers in loose clusters 10 inches tall. *Camassia*, 'Blue Danube', comes later, with lavender and violet flowers on 2-foot stalks. The flowers open from the bottom of the stem, a habit that makes *Camassia* a long-lasting bloomer.

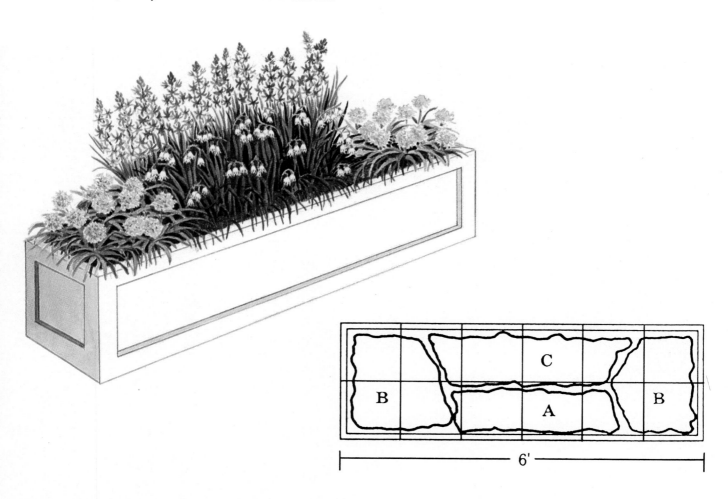

	COMMON NAME	VARIETY	SCIENTIFIC NAME	COLOR	HEIGHT	BLOOM	NUMBER OF BULBS
A	Snowflake	'Summer Snowflake'	*Leucojum aestivum*	White	1–1½ feet	April–May	12
B	Allium		*Allium moly*	Yellow	10 inches	April–May	24
C	Wild Hyacinth	'Blue Danube'	*Camassia leichtlinii*	Lavender-violet	2–3 feet	April–May	12

SPRING HARMONY

FLOWERING HERBS IN A BARREL

Here is a collection of five popular perennial herbs, chosen for their fragrance and flowers. Grow them in half a whiskey barrel (available at most garden supply stores—make sure they have drainage holes), or plant them in a circular bed, where the design can be enlarged to emphasize the contrast between the different herbs. For your greatest enjoyment, locate this garden near the kitchen door where you can appreciate the fragrance and easily use the flavorful leaves in cooking.

Flowering Herbs in a Barrel

FLOWERING HERBS IN A BARREL

	Common Name	Scientific Name	Color	Height	Bloom	Number of Plants
A	Lavender	*Lavendula*	Lavender with blue, gray	2½ feet	June–July	4
B	Borage	*Borago*	Blue	1½ feet	June–August	4
C	Catnip	*Nepeta cataria*	Purple	1½ feet	July–September	4
D	Chives	*Allium schoenoprasum*	Purple	2 feet	June	6
E	Sage	*Salvia officinalis*	Silver with green	1–2 feet	June	6

When planting from seed: Use 1 seed packet for each variety.

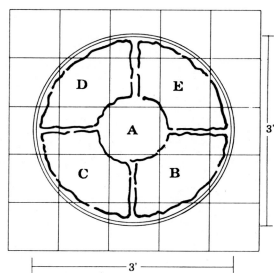

A LANDSCAPING PLAN FO

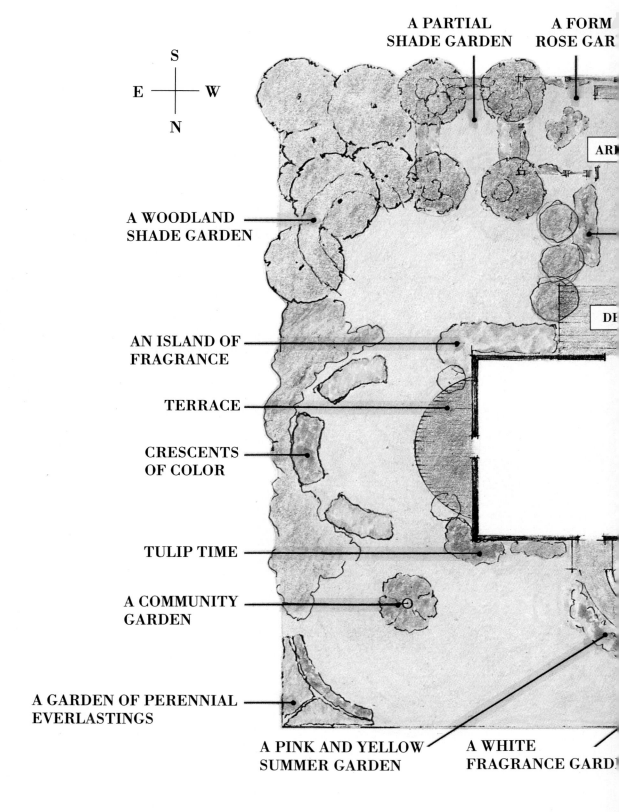

A PARTIAL SHADE GARDEN

A FORM ROSE GAR

S

E ✛ W

N

ARI

A WOODLAND SHADE GARDEN

AN ISLAND OF FRAGRANCE

DI

TERRACE

CRESCENTS OF COLOR

TULIP TIME

A COMMUNITY GARDEN

A GARDEN OF PERENNIAL EVERLASTINGS

A PINK AND YELLOW SUMMER GARDEN

A WHITE FRAGRANCE GARD

QUARTER-ACRE PLOT

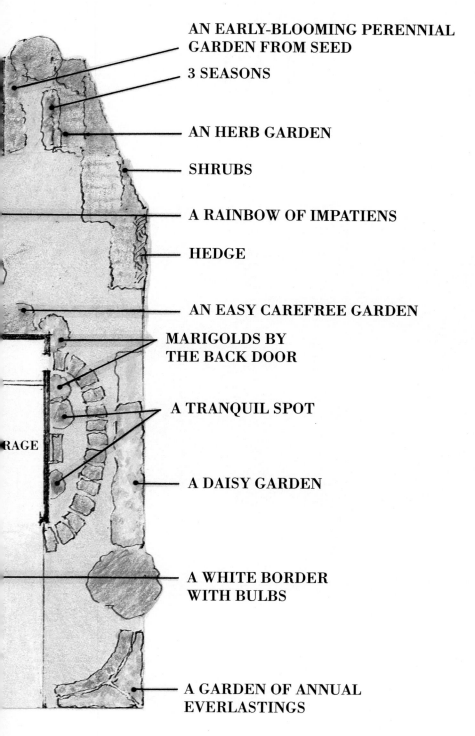

AN EARLY-BLOOMING PERENNIAL
GARDEN FROM SEED

3 SEASONS

AN HERB GARDEN

SHRUBS

A RAINBOW OF IMPATIENS

HEDGE

AN EASY CAREFREE GARDEN

MARIGOLDS BY
THE BACK DOOR

A TRANQUIL SPOT

RAGE

A DAISY GARDEN

A WHITE BORDER
WITH BULBS

A GARDEN OF ANNUAL
EVERLASTINGS

QUARTER ACRE PLOT

THE USDA PLANT HARDINESS MAP OF THE UNITED STATES

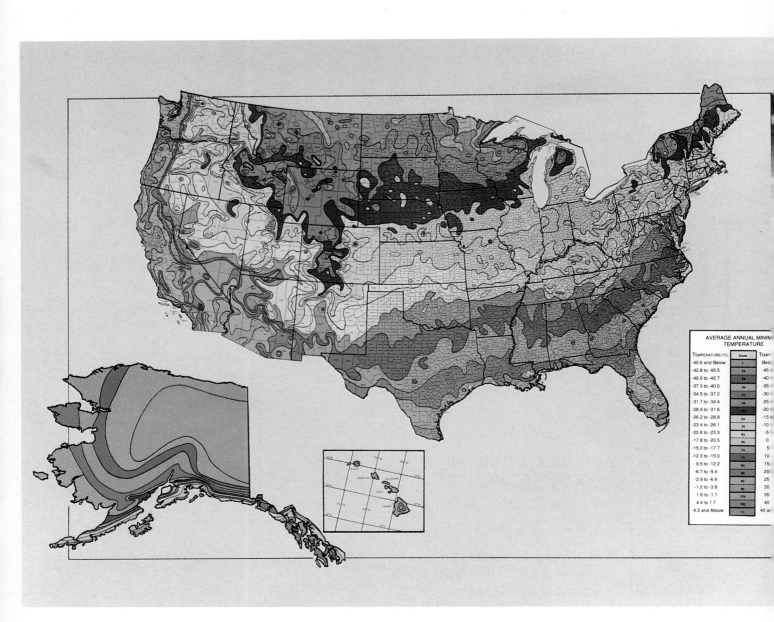

INDEX

(NOTE: Italicized page numbers refer to captions.)

Achillea, in everlastings garden, 79
Ageratum, 63
  in crescent garden, 18
  in partial shade garden, 58
  in shade garden, 34
Ajuga, to replace bulbs, 40
Allium, in spring bulb container garden, 89
Alyssum. *See Lobularia*
Amaryllis, hardy. *See Lycoris*
Anemone
  in early spring garden, 36
  in spring bulb garden, 39
Annual flower gardens, 11–31
  crescent shape, 17–23
  cutting garden, 24–26
  everlastings, 27–28
  fragrant, 15–16
  impatiens garden, 29
  low maintenance, 12–14
  marigold garden, 30–31
Anthemis, in daisy garden, 76
Aquilegia, 7, 61
Artemisia
  in ornamental grasses garden, 83
  in pink and yellow garden, 74
Aster, annual. *See Callistephus*
Aster, 65
  in autumn garden, 81
  in daisy garden, 76
  in "tranquil spot," 64
Astilbe, in shade garden, 57
Aurinia, in daisy garden, 76
Autumn garden for townhouse, plants for, 82 (chart)
Baby's breath. *See Gypsophila*
Bachelor's button. *See Centaurea*
Balance, as a design principle, 8
Bee balm. *See Monarda*
Begonia, 8
  in partial shade garden, 58
  in shade garden, 34

in woodland shade garden, 60
Bells of Ireland. *See Molucella*
Bergenia, 65
  in "tranquil spot," 64
Bleeding heart. *See Dicentra*
Blue and yellow crescent garden, plants for, 19 (chart)
Bluebells. *See Phacelia*
Blue crescent garden, plants for, 21 (chart)
Blue fescue. *See Feustuca*
Blue lace flower. *See Trachymene*
Border mum. *See Chrysanthemum*
Browallia, in partial shade garden, 58
Buddleia, in white fragrance garden, 67
Bulb flower gardens, 33–49
  colorful spring bulbs, 39
  in community setting, 44
  daffodil garden, 38
  for early spring, 36–37
  fall-blooming bulb garden, 49
  oriental, 40
  pattern garden, 42–43
  sitting garden, 34–35
  summer bulb garden, 47–48
  tulip garden, 41
  white border with bulbs, 45–46
Butterfly bush. *See Buddleia*
Butterfly gladiolus. *See Gladiolus*
Caladium, 48
  in summer bulb garden, 47
  in white border garden, 45
  in woodland shade garden, 60
Callas, in white border garden, 45
Callistephus, 26
  in crescent garden, 18, 20, 22
  in cutting garden, 24
Camassia, in spring bulb container garden, 89
Candytuft. *See Iberis*
Catalog, to receive from Burpee, 9
Centaurea, 14
  in annual garden, 12
  in crescent garden, 20
Ceratostigma, in fall-blooming bulb garden, 49

Chamomile, in herb garden, 70
Chrysanthemum
  in autumn garden, 81
  in daisy garden, 76
Cleome, 11, 14
  in annual garden, 12
Colchicum, in fall-blooming bulb garden, 49
Coleus
  in partial shade garden, 58
  in sitting garden, 34
Columbine. *See Aquilegia*
Combination gardens, 63–71
  herb garden, 70–71
  salad garden, 68–69
  in "tranquil spot," 64–66
  white fragrant garden, 67
Community garden, plants for, 44 (chart)
Container gardens, 85–91
  daffodil garden, 86
  flowering herbs, 90–91
  spring bulb garden, 89
  tulip garden, 87–88
Coralbells, 7
Coreopsis, 63
  in pink and yellow garden, 74
Cornflower. *See Centaurea*
Cosmos, 14, 26, 63
  in annual garden, 12
  in crescent garden, 18
  in cutting garden, 24
Crocus
  in early spring garden, 36
  in fall-blooming bulb garden, 49
  in white border garden, 45
Cutting garden, plants for, 25 (chart)
Daffodil. *See also Narcissus*
  daffodil container garden, plants for, 86 (chart)
  daffodil garden, plants for, 38 (chart)
Dahlia, 48
  in summer bulb garden, 47
Daisy garden, plants for, 77 (chart)
Daylily, 63
Deadheading
  annuals, 11
  tagetes, 12
Design plans
  autumn garden for townhouse, 82
  combination garden in "tranquil spot", 66

community garden, 44
crescent garden, 17, 19, 21, 23
cutting garden, 25
daffodil container garden, 86
daffodil garden, 38
daisy garden, 76
early-blooming perennial garden from seed, 78
early spring garden, 37
English pattern garden (bulbs), 43
everlastings garden
  -annual, 28
  perennial, 80
fall-blooming bulb garden, 49
fragrant garden, 16
herb container garden, 91
herb garden, 71
impatiens garden, 29
low maintenance garden, 13
marigold garden, 31
oriental bulb garden, 40
ornamental grasses garden, 83
partial shade garden, 59
pink and yellow garden, 75
quarter-acre plot, landscaping, 92
rose garden at end of lawn, 53
rose garden (formal), 55
salad garden, 69
scale, 9
sitting garden (bulbs), 34
spring bulb container garden, 89
summer bulb garden, 48
tulip container garden, 88
tulip garden, 41
white border garden with bulbs, 46
white fragrance garden, 67
woodland shade garden, 61
Design principles, 7–8
Dianthus, 26
  in cutting garden, 24
  in pink and yellow garden, 74
Dicentra, 61
  in all-white garden, 46
Dill, in salad garden, 68
Drainage, in garden planning, 9
Drying flowers, 27
Dusty miller, 63
  in white border garden, 45

Early-blooming perennial garden, plants for, 78 (chart)
English pattern garden, plants for, 43 (chart)
Eranthis, in early spring garden, 36
Euonymous, to replace bulbs, 40
Everlastings garden
  annual, plants for, 28 (chart)
  perennial, plants for, 80 (chart)
Exposure. *See Location*
Fall-blooming bulb garden, plants for, 49 (chart)
Feustuca, in everlastings garden, 79
Flowering maple. *See Maple, flowering*
Flowering tobacco. *See Nicotiana*
Focal point, as a design principle, 8
Fragrant garden
  plants for, 16 (chart)
  white, 67
Gaillardia, in daisy garden, 76
Galanthus
  in early spring garden, 36
  in oriental bulb garden, 40
Gardening Hot Line, for customer questions, 9
Garden plans. *See Design plans*
Geranium, 61
  in community garden, 44
  in container garden, 85
Gladiolus, 48
  in summer bulb garden, 47
  in white border garden, 45
Globe amaranth. *See Gomphrena*
Gomphrena, as everlastings, 27
Grape hyacinth. *See Muscari*
Gypsophila, 26
  in crescent garden, 20, 22
  in cutting garden, 24
  in everlastings garden, 79
Helichrysum, as everlastings, 27
Helictotrichon, in ornamental grasses garden, 83
Heliopsis, in daisy garden, 76

Herb container garden, plants for, 91 (chart)
Herb garden, plants for, 71 (chart)
Hosta, in shade garden, 57
Hot Line, Gardening, for customer questions, 9
Houseplants, outdoors in summer, 7
Hyacinth. *See Hyacinthus*
Hyacinthus, 33
  in community garden, 44
  in white border garden, 45
  in white fragrance garden, 67
Hydrangea, in container garden, 85
Iberis
  in all-white garden, *46*
  in rose garden, 54
Immortelle. *See Xeranthemum*
Impatiens, *8*
  in partial shade garden, 58
  in shade garden, 57
  in sitting garden, 34
Impatiens garden, colors for, 29 (chart)
Iris, *63*
  in early spring garden, 36
Landscaping plan, for quarter-acre plot, 92–93
Lavender. *See Lavendula*
Lavendula, 65
  against wall, 64
Layout, factors to be considered in, 7
Leadwort. *See Ceratostigma*
Lettuce, in salad garden, 68
Leucojum, in spring bulb container garden, 89
Lilium, 48
  in summer bulb garden, 47
  in white border garden, 45
  in white fragrance garden, 67
Lily. *See Lilium*
Lily turf. *See Liriope*
Limonium
  as everlastings, 27
  in everlastings garden, perennial, 79
Liriope, *48*, 61
  in summer bulb garden, 47
Lobularia
  in community garden, 44

in crescent garden, 22
  for fragrance, 15
Location, in garden planning, 9
Loosestrife. *See Lythrum*
Love-in-a-mist. *See Nigella*
Low maintenance garden, plants for, 13 (chart)
Lupine. *See Lupinus*
Lupinus, 7
Lycoris, 48
  in summer bulb garden, 47
  in white fragrance garden, 67
Lythrum, 65
  in pink and yellow garden, 74
  in "tranquil spot," 64
Maiden grass. *See Miscanthus*
Maintenance, time considerations in planning, 8
Maple, flowering, in partial shade garden, 58
Marigold. *See also Tagetes*
  Marigold garden, plants for, 31 (chart)
Mathiola, for fragrance, 15
Mignonette. *See Reseda*
Miscanthus, in pink and yellow garden, *74*
Mock orange. *See Philadelphus*
Molucella, as everlastings, 27
Monarda, in pink and yellow garden, *74*
Muscari, in oriental bulb garden, 40
Narcissus, *33*, 35
  in shade garden, 34
  in white border garden, 45
  in white fragrance garden, 67
Narcissus container garden, plants for, 86 (chart)
Narcissus garden, plants for, 38 (chart)
Nasturtium. *See Tropaeolum*
Nepeta, to replace bulbs, 40
Nicotiana, *11*
  in crescent garden, 22
  for fragrance, 15
  in partial shade garden, 58
  in white fragrance garden, 67
Nigella, as everlastings, 27

Oriental bulb garden, plants for, 40 (chart)
Ornamental grasses garden, plants for, 83 (chart)
Paeonia, in daisy garden, 76
Pansy, in shade garden, 57
Partial shade garden, plants for, 59 (chart)
Peony. *See Paeonia*
Perennial gardens, 73–83
  autumn garden for townhouse, 81–82
  daisy garden, 76–77
  early-blooming from seed, 78
  everlastings, 79–80
  ornamental grasses, 83
  pink and yellow, 74–75
Petunia, in container garden, 85
Phacelia, in crescent garden, 20
Philadelphus, in white fragrance garden, 67
Phlox, for fragrance, 15
Pincushion flower. *See Scabiosa*
Pink and yellow garden, plants for, 75 (chart)
Pink crescent garden, plants for, 23 (chart)
Pinks. *See Dianthus*
Plans. *See* Design plans
Plumbago, to replace bulbs, 40
Polianthes, 48
  in summer bulb garden, 47
Proportion, as a design principle, 7
Puschkinia, in early spring garden, 36
Queen Anne's lace, *63*
Radish, in salad garden, 68
Reseda, for fragrance, 15
Rhythm, as a design principle, 8
Rose gardens, 51–55
  at end of lawn, 52–53
  plants for, 53 (chart)
  formal, 54–55
  plants for, 55 (chart)
Rudbeckia, in daisy garden, 76
Salad garden, plants for, 69 (chart)
Salvia, *11*
  in community garden, 44
  in crescent garden, 20
  in everlastings garden, 79

in partial shade garden, 58
Satureja, in herb garden, 70
Scabiosa, 26
  as everlastings, 27
Scale, as a design principle, 7
Scilla
  in daffodil container garden, 86
  in tulip container garden, 87
  in tulip garden, 41
Sedum, 65
  in autumn garden, 81
  in everlastings garden, 79
  in fall-blooming bulb garden, 49
  in pink and yellow garden, *74*
  in "tranquil spot," 64
Seed, perennial garden from, 78
Seedlings
  thinning, 11
  transplanting, 11
Seeds, starting indoors, 11
Sesleria, in ornamental grasses garden, 83
Shade gardens, 57–61
  partial shade, 58–59
  woodland shade, 60–61
Sitting garden (bulbs), plants for, 35 (chart)
Snapdragons, *11*
Snowdrops. *See Galanthus*
Spring bulb container garden, plants for, 89 (chart)
Spring bulb garden
  colorful, plants for, 39 (chart)
  early, plants for, 37 (chart)
Starflower. *See Scabiosa*
Statice. *See Limonium*
Stock. *See Mathiola*
Stonecrop. *See Sedum*
Strawflower. *See Helichrysum*
Summer bulb garden, plants for, 48 (chart)
Summer savory. *See Satureja*
Sunlight, in garden planning, 9
Tagetes, *14*, *26*
  in crescent garden, 18
  in cutting garden, 24
Tagetes garden, plants for, 31 (chart)
Thinning seedlings. *See Seedlings*

Tomato, in salad garden, 68
Townhouse garden, 81–82
Trachymene, *26*
  in crescent garden, 18
Transplanting seedlings. *See* Seedlings
Tropaeolum, *14*
  bloom time, 12
  for fragrance, 15
  in salad, 12
  in salad garden, 68
  sowing seed, 11
Tuberose. *See Polianthes*
Tulip. *See also Tulipa*
  container garden, plants for, 88 (chart)
  garden, plants for, 41 (chart)
Tulipa, *33*, 65
  in all-white garden, *46*
  in community garden, 44
  in oriental bulb garden, 40
  in spring bulb garden, 39
  in "tranquil spot," 64
Tulipa container garden, plants for, 88 (chart)
Tulipa garden, plants for, 41 (chart)
Unity, as a design principle, 8
USDA plant hardiness map, 94
Verbena, *11*
Vinca, 35
  in sitting garden, 34
White garden
  border with bulbs, plants for, 46 (chart)
  fragrant, plants for, 67 (chart)
Windflower. *See Anemone*
Winter aconite. *See Eranthis*
Wood hyacinth. *See Scilla*
Woodland shade garden, plants for, 61 (chart)
Xeranthemum, as everlastings, 27
Yarrow. *See Achillea*
Yellow and blue crescent garden, plants for, 19 (chart)
Yellow and pink garden, plants for, 75 (chart)
Zinnia, *14*, *26*
  in annual garden, 12
  in crescent garden, 18, 22
  in cutting garden, 24
  in daisy garden, 76